DESTINED FOR GLORY

The Meaning of Suffering

MARGARET CLARKSON

William B. Eerdmans Publishing Company

*To the Nowack family,
and especially to Julie,
in loving memory of Jean and Carl*

Copyright © 1983 by Wm. B. Eerdmans Publishing Co.
255 Jefferson Ave. S.E., Grand Rapids, Mich. 49503
All rights reserved
Printed in the United States of America

Reprinted, April 1984

Library of Congress Cataloging in Publication Data:

Clarkson, Edith Margaret, 1915-
Destined for glory.

1. Suffering — Religious aspects — Christianity.
I. Title.
BT732.7.C53 1983   231'.8   83-1704

ISBN 0-8028-3601-1

All biblical references in this work are taken from the New International
Version of the Bible unless otherwise indicated.

Holy Bible: New International Version. Copyright © 1978 by the New York
International Bible Society. Used by permission of Zondervan Bible
Publishers.

Gratitude is expressed to MOODY MONTHLY for kind permission to use
some of the material in Chapters 23, 31, and 32 that first appeared in its
pages.

CONTENTS

FOREWORD

IF YOU WERE TO MEET MARGARET CLARKSON IT MIGHT never occur to you that you were meeting a life-long sufferer. Margaret doesn't come across that way. The intensity and variety of her enthusiasms, the sparkle in her eyes, and the no-nonsense vigor of her humor are what would impress you. Perhaps it is fitting, then, that she should pull aside the veil and let us know in her preface that all she has learned she has learned as a result of her personal grappling with pain.

No one who has not suffered could write as she does, and because of this we should all be grateful for the fruits of Margaret's suffering. If the Son of Man had to "learn obedience through the things that he suffered" it must logically follow that to triumph as He triumphed we must learn the same lessons in the same way. Tragically, we live in a day that measures faith by the absence of suffering and looks to divine miracles as a proof of genuine faith.

Miracles are to authenticate God's messages and to awaken our awe and reverence before Him. They are not to vindicate our personal faith. It is not by miraculous deliverance that our faith grows but by discovering His faithfulness in the midst of our pain. This is the kind of lesson that Margaret Clarkson's book so clearly teaches. It has moved me to a greater awareness of the struggle we are engaged in and I for one thank God for what she has to say.

John White

TESTAMENT TO TRUTH

WHY HAVE I TRIED TO WRITE A BOOK ON THE MEANING OF suffering, you may wonder? The answer is very simple—basically because of my own necessity, and the Holy Spirit's ministry to me through the Word of God. I know whereof I speak.

My mother has told me that my first words were "My head hurts!" I can well believe it. I can't remember a time when I was not tormented by excruciating headaches coupled with convulsive vomiting, lasting for days at a time. They have effectively marked my whole life with their cruel and ruthless impress, and remain a problem to this day.

When I was three years old, I spent most of a year in bed with what is now known as juvenile arthritis. I can still remember the pain, the sleepless nights, the inability to move without screaming, the bald spot worn on the back of my head after I lay so long in bed. I had to learn to walk all over again when I recovered. A second arthritic attack when I was twelve settled in one arm, leaving my wrist and hand swollen and partly crippled for several years. As I emerged from adolescence, however, arthritis receded into the background, as childhood arthritis often does, and I was left with only the headaches and a congenital back problem to contend with.

Unknown to anyone, from birth I had had a slight malformation in the lower spine, its discomfort, though real, being masked by the greater pain of the headaches. By the time I was fifty, increasing pain and spasm coupled with difficulty in walking concentrated attention on this, and surgery followed. The benefits of the spinal fusion were just becoming evident about three years later when the arthritis moved back into prominence, as juvenile arthritis tends to do in mid-life. It spread rapidly, attacking almost all my joints, including my spine, and forcing me into an early retirement. It continues to be a major problem.

I was born into a loveless and unhappy marriage which finally broke up when I was about twelve. My most outstanding memories are of tension, fear, insecurity, upset, and isolation, along with the inevitable guilt feelings which sensitive children assume when caught up in undercurrents beyond their understanding. I struggled alone with my anxiety, my alienation, and my despair, never voicing them to anyone. Who was there to tell? The social sciences were not then developed as they are today, and the adults in my life were too overwhelmed by their own troubles to pay any serious attention to mine.

Burdened with illness and the financial problems common to broken homes, and coming into the labor market during the worst years of the Great Depression, I found that a university education was not a possibility for me. I began to teach elementary school in 1935 when I was barely twenty, with only one year of post-secondary training. I had to go to the far north of Ontario to find work at all, and spent seven long, lonely years in areas remote from Christian fellowship before I was able to return to teach in my home city of Toronto.

For thirty-eight long, hard years I taught in a variety of school situations, loving my work, but struggling with pain and illness every inch of the way. Today, although increasingly handicapped and never free from pain, I count myself blessed that I no longer have to fight for daily survival as I did during my years in the work force.

Strange to relate, we attended a good church in my childhood. There I became a Christian when I encountered John Bunyan in *Pilgrim's Progress* at the age of ten. From then on I studied my Bible and read my hymnbook daily. Child though I was, I began to search the Scriptures for light on the imponderable questions that haunted me; gradually, over the years, I came to know the gentle ministry of the Holy Spirit in this regard.

But life was hard. It was not easy to accept the limitations that had been laid upon me. No part of my personality escaped their devastation. A pain-filled body is a heavy burden for a young person with an active mind to bear, even without the trauma of an unhappy home. I was different from everyone I knew. I couldn't do what others my age did. I didn't fit in anywhere. Helplessness, hopelessness, rage, frustration, despair, the compulsion to give up and seek cessation of pain in the darkness of death — I knew them all. Despite the reality of a Christian commitment from which I never wavered for a moment, I spent years struggling to find any real meaning in life as I had to live it. How well I know the "Why?" of human anguish!

I found my answers in the Word of God, but not before I was well into my forties, and not without much pain. Slowly but surely the Holy Spirit began to make real to me the teaching of the Scriptures concerning the sovereignty of God and its meaning for my life. Gradually I came to understand something of God's over-arching purpose for His children and His ways of bringing it about. Slowly I began to learn to look beyond my immediate situation to God's ultimate purpose for my life, and doing so I gradually found peace. As my knowledge and understanding of the Scriptures increased, so did my assurance and my spiritual growth.

My general health remains unchanged to this day. Despite their best efforts, my doctors have never been able to do much for me beyond offering palliative measures for my illnesses and giving me much-appreciated moral support. Though I have besought God earnestly for healing, He has not seen fit to touch my body with a miracle. His working in me has been more intimate, more eternal — He has touched my spirit and is working His miracle of healing there.

I have learned that through understanding of the Scriptures there is comfort and hope in human sorrow. Never before have I put into print the personal experiences of which I am writing now; indeed, my closest friends know little if anything about them. It is only with the greatest reluctance that I disclose them now. But how else could I validate the truths of which I am writing? God's truth as revealed in the Scriptures has saved my life from destruction, and my spirit from death. This book is my testament to the power of God's sovereignty and to His faithfulness to those who will rest their measure of life's sorrows on His inviolable Word. I realize that many of my readers will know sufferings far greater than anything I have experienced; I offer these pages in the assurance that God's truth embraces the totality of human pain, in whatever form it may appear.

I make no attempt to be philosophical in this book. There may be sufferers who can be helped by a philosophical treatise, but I am not one of them. I doubt that many sufferers are. C. S. Lewis's philosophical book on the subject, *The Problem of Pain,* while beautiful and moving, is remote; by his own admission he had had little personal experience of suffering when he wrote it. Twenty years later, the book he wrote following the death of his wife, *A Grief Observed,* was anything but philosophical — it was a cry of human anguish which only faith could assuage.

And I approach the Scriptures in faith. We do not have to understand everything about God's sovereignty in order to prove its power. Many topics I have touched on could be reasoned out more fully, but I doubt that that would be of any advantage to the sufferer. Yet I find that while much of the Scriptural teaching about suffering may call primarily for faith rather than for reason, nonetheless it satisfies my mind. There is no dichotomy between faith and reason; God's Word is eminently reasonable.

I could wish that I had come to an understanding of the biblical truths that have brought me healing and freedom much earlier in life than I did; I might have been spared years of spiritual poverty and loss. My first hope in offering this book is that by making available clearly and concisely the teachings that I was so long in gathering together, other long-term sufferers may be spared wasted years and needless anguish. My second hope is that it may help other Christians to understand what the Scriptures really teach about suffering so that when trouble comes to them they may be prepared and be able to work together with God to allow Him to fulfill His purposes in their sorrow.

When this manuscript was little more than half written, I had a visit from my young friend Julie, eldest daughter of the family of whom I write in my opening chapter. Five years earlier she had lost her widowed mother after a painful struggle with cancer which had lasted nine years. As she read my manuscript she began to question me closely, and we spent three days discussing in depth the biblical teachings about suffering and evil. Many unresolved conflicts concerning her mother's death came to the surface, and we talked them out. She was able to find rest on a number of points that had been troubling her and commit herself in a new way to God's sovereignty.

Two weeks later I received her thank-you note, and with it, devastating news. During a routine physical examination required by her school board, she had found that she, too, was a victim of cancer.

During the months of surgery, chemotherapy, and radiation

treatments that followed, she told me how grateful she was that God had prepared her for her trouble by giving her a more thorough biblical understanding of the whole problem of human pain than she had had at the time of her mother's illness and death.

"After going through what I did watching Mom's suffering, and having so many questions still in my mind about it," she wrote me, "I think I would simply have fallen apart at my own diagnosis if God hadn't given me those days with you, learning about God's purpose in pain.

"Now I know for sure that God is in control of my life. He knew what was coming, and He sent me the help I needed before I even knew I needed it. I am resting in His sovereignty now, and trusting Him to use this evil to work out His highest purpose for my life."

What higher ministry could one hope for in writing a book — or living a life?

SOVEREIGN LORD!

O Father, You are sovereign
  In all the worlds You made;
Your mighty Word was spoken,
  And light and life obeyed.
Your voice commands the seasons
  And bounds the ocean's shore,
Sets stars within their courses
  And stills the tempests' roar.

O Father, You are sovereign
  In all affairs of man;
No powers of death or darkness
  Can thwart Your perfect plan.
All chance and change
    transcending,
  Supreme in time and space,
You hold Your trusting children
  Secure in Your embrace.

O Father, You are sovereign,
  The Lord of human pain,
Transmuting earthly sorrows
  To gold of heavenly gain,
All evil overruling,
  As none but Conqueror could,
Your love pursues its purpose —
  Our souls' eternal good.

O Father, You are sovereign!
  We see You darkly now,
But soon before Your triumph
  Earth's every knee shall bow.
With this glad hope before us
  Our faith springs forth anew:
Our Sovereign Lord and Savior,
  We trust and worship You!

MARGARET CLARKSON

• I •

THE PATH OF THE JUST

JEAN GOT THE MESSAGE BY PHONE THAT BLUE-AND-GOLD spring morning. Carl had had a stroke at the hospital where he was a chaplain. The doctors were not at all sure that he could survive the open-heart surgery that was his only hope, but they wanted her permission to try it. Might they go ahead? Numbly, she consented. So it had come at last!

All her married life Jean had known that some day she would be left to raise her children alone. Carl had had to spend six years in bed as a child. Rheumatic fever had damaged his heart so severely that he had never been able to lead a normal life. Much of his education had had to be given at home. His heart beat so violently that only by walking backwards, very slowly, could he go up stairs; its throbbing was always visible in his forehead and throat. But he was blessed with a brilliant mind and a sunny personality. He did well in his studies, and everyone who knew him loved him.

He was in graduate school at a Christian college when he met Jean, then an undergraduate. Before long they had fallen in love. "I know I'll be left a widow with a young family to care for," Jean told me when she asked me to play for their wedding. "But I'd rather live part of my life with Carl than the rest of my life without him!"

I understood her attitude when I met Carl. He had a radiancy, a transparency, a beauty of holiness combined with a humorous *joie de vivre* such as I have seldom encountered. Although I was much older than either of them, I delighted Jean by commenting wryly, "It's lucky for you that you met him first!"

They were married when she finished college. She taught while he took a second master's degree, this time in theology. Then they settled into a semi-rural pastorate near his family home. Before many years had passed, they were the happy parents of three daughters and a son.

1

Carl loved his work, though it taxed his always-precarious health to the limit. But God's blessing was evident in his ministry. His long years of suffering had endowed him with spiritual insights which proved invaluable in the pastorate. His people loved him deeply.

And they loved Jean just as dearly. Gifted and creative, she had a warm, vibrant personality and infectious gaiety, coupled with a keen spiritual sensitivity, that made her a joy to know. She was already a skilled teacher; rapidly she became a superb mother and a beloved pastor's wife. God used her ministry as much as Carl's as they served their quiet community faithfully for eleven years.

But Carl's heart condition steadily worsened. Eventually he realized that he must leave the active ministry and seek work less physically demanding. He began a course to train as a hospital chaplain.

The family moved to the suburbs of a large industrial city where the children would find better educational opportunities. While Carl completed his training they lived frugally on what little they had been able to save from his small salary as a rural pastor. After graduation he did maintenance work at the hospital where he had studied, and later, when a chaplaincy vacancy arose, he joined its staff. Since he had always lived with the frustrations of a sharply restricted life, he was specially equipped to help others accept the limitations of illness. Having spent most of his own life under the shadow of death, he was able to minister profoundly to those appointed to die. Before long he was the chaplain most sought after by patients and hospital staff alike. And now his own life hung in the balance.

Miraculously, Carl survived his surgery. He was told he must rest a full year following his release from the hospital, so Jean applied for a teaching position. She secured an appointment for September in the suburb where they lived. By then Carl would be home from hospital, and he and the children, aged eight to four-teen, could look after one another while Jean was at school.

Together the family rejoiced that God had spared Carl and given Jean work to meet their needs during his enforced idleness. Jean had loved teaching — she would enjoy being back in the schoolroom. Better still, her starting salary would be considerably higher than her husband's stipend had ever been. Four growing children and Carl's three years of training and his illness had made many financial demands. How graciously God was caring for them, they said, as they thanked Him for His faithfulness!

In August Jean went up for the routine physical examination required by her school board — and lost a breast and four ribs after cancer was discovered. Both parents were now in the hospital, and the family had no income at all.

The weeks that followed were difficult ones. Carl's faith had been tested over a lifetime and stood firm, but Jean was deeply shaken. She had known nothing but radiant good health and boundless energy all her life. She had learned to come to terms with Carl's disability, but her own pain and weakness were new and bitter hardships. Standing up to psychological suffering was one thing, she discovered; learning to endure personal pain was quite another.

Her faith was sorely tried. Though she had always known that she might lose Carl, it had never occurred to her that her own vibrant life might be cut short. How could God allow both father and mother in one family to be so stricken? There were no grandparents on either side. Jean had no relatives. Carl was one of a large but widely scattered family, several of them missionaries in distant countries. Who was there to help? Surely God was asking too much of one family! Thus Jean poured out her complaints before God in the bitterness of her soul.

Eventually faith triumphed. Carl was able to minister to his wife, and gradually she was enabled to fling herself afresh on the faithfulness of God. The children's faith grew as they watched their parents' increasing confidence in God. Together the family prayed and trusted and watched Him work. Financial assistance came in from a variety of sources, all of them unexpected and some of them never identified. By Christmas Carl was working a shortened day at light hospital duties. In January Jean began to teach. God had seen them through their night of crisis.

For three and a half years, things moved along smoothly enough on the surface, though always there was the undercurrent of strain. Jean continued to teach. The children took over most of the housekeeping. Carl carried on his work as a chaplain, though with increasing difficulty. The hospital employed the girls in various capacities during school vacations.

Then one December noon, Carl came out of a hospital room

in which he had been visiting a patient, experienced a massive stroke, and was gone in an instant.

Jean was now the sole support of the family.

A year later, just six months before her anticipated five-year cancer-free check-up, she received chilling news. The cancer had not been stopped. All that could be done now was to try to slow its spread with more surgery and the use of experimental drugs.

Who can tell what anguish Jean must have known as she faced the fact that she must leave her children alone in the world before they were able to fend for themselves? What must have been her grief, not only to witness but to be forced to contribute to the overshadowing of their lives with sorrows and a burden of responsibilities too great for their young shoulders? Why should innocent children have to suffer such trauma? Many were the struggles and waverings and depths of depression that Jean experienced as her suffering and weakness increased; but in the end, faith triumphed. Gradually she grew in spiritual strength. God's peace and the reality of His presence were evident to all who knew her, and she became a powerful witness to His sustaining grace.

Sheer necessity forced her to continue teaching, despite her growing pain and difficulties. Stephen, her youngest, was now in eighth grade; Liz and Mary Robin, the two younger girls, were in high school. The eldest daughter, Julie, was in college. The goal towards which Jean was driving herself so relentlessly was to see at least some of her family through school, into jobs, and able to help the others before she died.

And, fighting every inch of the way, Jean attained her purpose. Julie graduated and found work close enough to home that she could live with her mother and help her. By now Liz and Mary Robin were away at college.

Jean was still teaching when Liz graduated in June and Mary finished her sophomore year. Stephen had only one more year in high school. Jean was coming close to realizing her dream of seeing her children self-sufficient. Then one morning in early July, she did not awaken. Her long, hard battle with cancer was ended. The children were alone.

Why should one family have to suffer so deeply? Carl and Jean were a profoundly Christian couple. Their one aim in life was to know Christ and to make Him known. They spent their lives in selfless service to others. Countless people will long remember them for the richness of their spiritual ministry. The reality of their Christian experience was such that despite their shadowed childhood, all four children have made their parents' beliefs the basis of their own lives and continue in them to this day. Should not such faith and commitment know better reward than the devastation this family has had to experience?

Why? Why? Why? Why? Which of us cannot draw from our own circle of acquaintances all too many illustrations of the problem of undeserved suffering? What has Christianity to say in the face of human anguish?

• 2 •
WHY?

WHY DO THE RIGHTEOUS SUFFER? THIS IS THE QUESTION WITH
which Job wrestled in antiquity. This is the question with which
mankind has struggled ever since. This is our question today.

Why is there such suffering in our world? Why is evil so
strong? If God is all-powerful, why does wrong seem so often to
triumph? If God is not only powerful but good, why does He allow
pain to afflict His creation?

That God is, indeed, both good and powerful is one of the
basic tenets of Christian belief. Therefore there must be an answer
to the problem of pain, and it must be a Christian answer. But it
is not an easy question, and it does not admit of any easy answers.
Surely Christians, of all people, ought to be able to speak peace to
our aching world. Yet what do we find today? Most Christians
seem to be as baffled as anyone else by the enigma of suffering.
Few of us have learned to triumph over it in our own lives. We
speak to the question with a diversity of voices.

Some answer with humanistic philosophies, much as the
world does. Some assume a fatalistic attitude, or a stoical one.
Some refuse to face the issue. Some resort to a Pollyannaish attitude; others take refuge in a pie-in-the-sky escapism and never
really come to grips with the facts. Many seek their answers in
counselling, psychology, or a variety of self-help theories.

Some think that Christians are exempt from trouble in this
world and preach inviting but unsubstantiated doctrines of instant
health, wealth, and happiness in Jesus. Some teach that physical
healing is a part of the Atonement, and that anyone who is sick
is either lacking in faith, out of God's will, or harboring some
secret sin. Others seek miraculous deliverance from all of life's
difficulties and spend their lives running from one source of hoped-
for miracle to another. Some are so shaken when trouble strikes or
miracles are not forthcoming that they become bitter and cold;
some even abandon their Christian faith. None of these responses

6

to suffering rightly commends the power of the Gospel to an unbelieving world.

Some Christians, it is true, do stand up to their trials with courage and God-honoring commitment and composure, thus giving true witness to the reality of the faith they profess. But sad to say, this does not seem to be the response of most evangelical Christians today in the face of adversity. Why does our Christian trumpet give forth such an uncertain sound to an anguished world?

May not the most probable reason be that most of us, clergy and laity alike, have never seriously set ourselves to discover what the Scriptures really teach about suffering? The mighty doctrines that alone can shed compelling light on human sorrow are largely neglected today. They are seldom taught in our seminaries, preached from our pulpits, or considered in our Bible teaching. They are given scant attention in our Christian publications. We are satisfied with lesser things today. Most of us are content to deal largely in superficialities. To paraphrase G. K. Chesterton's comment about Christianity, the teaching of the Word of God concerning suffering has not been tried and found wanting — it has been found difficult and not tried.

We do not study the Scriptures closely enough to discern God's vast, over-arching purposes, reaching from eternity past, through time, and on to eternity yet to come. We have not sought to find our place — and the place of suffering — in His eternal plan. When trouble comes, we do not search out the whole counsel of God to sustain us. Rather, we seek to fortify ourselves with comforting passages of Scripture, with isolated promises, or with "proof" texts. If these do not support us, we crumble. No wonder we have so little to say to an unbelieving world about a problem as overwhelming as the problem of evil!

The Word of God *does* have answers to the problem of human pain, difficult as that problem is. They will not be found without much searching, but if we are willing to seek them diligently, we shall find them. We may not discover all the answers we should like to have, but we shall find all we really need to know.

The purpose of this book is to look into the Scriptures to see what they really have to say about the problem of suffering. But first, let's define the word itself. What is pain?

• 3 •
WHAT IS PAIN?

WHAT DO WE MEAN WHEN WE SPEAK OF THE PROBLEM OF pain? Most of us think at once of bodily pain, of illness, weakness, or physical suffering. This is indeed a large part of the problem of pain, but it is far from all of it. Human suffering is vastly greater than physical pain, terrible indeed as that can be.

The problem of pain embraces every area of evil known to man; it wears a thousand guises. If there are answers to human suffering, they must be great enough to include them all. For there are countless sorrows that can cripple the human spirit just as certainly as physical pain can cripple the human body.

There is psychological pain. There is the pain of circumstances that can't be changed, the pressure of which can gradually paralyze personality and productivity. There is the pain of being locked into life-situations that must be kept hidden from others, secret sorrows that may range in intensity from distressing to agonizing. There is the pain of unrelieved and unbearable tension. There is the pain of physical disability that may overshadow a whole lifetime, working its devastation in the deepest recesses of the personality and being.

There is the pain of disappointing relationships, of family breakdown, of alienation, of inability to relate to or communicate with others, of enduring spiritual or physical isolation. There is the pain of being unappreciated or misunderstood, of humiliation, injustice, selfishness, lust, or greed. There is the pain of a warped or twisted mind or personality.

There is the pain of unmet goals, of unrealized potential or creativity, of unrecognized worth, of unrewarded service, of unrequited love. There is the pain of living with unending frustration, the pain of physical deformity or disfigurement. There is the pain of anxiety, of haunting fear, or remorse. There is the pain of deep mental depression, of emotional instability or breakdown. There is the pain that rises from a troubled unconscious. There is the specter of suicide.

There is the pain of an unfulfilling or unhappy marriage, of sexual deprivation, abuse, or perversion. There is the pain of undesired singleness, widowhood, divorce, childlessness, homosexual orientation. There is the pain of watching our children choose the ways of folly over the ways of God, of seeing them become aloof, cool, hostile. There is the pain of murder, rape, cruelty, revenge.

There is the pain of having (or being) a physically handicapped child or a retarded one, or of watching innocent children suffer or die. There is the pain of childhood trauma, of broken homes. There is the pain of losing a beloved parent or marriage partner. There is the pain of pathetic and loveless old age, of senility.

There is the pain of poverty, or hunger, of loss of livelihood, of inability to work or to secure employment. There is the pain of sudden calamity, whether from accident, economic collapse, or some form of natural disaster. There is the unspeakable horror of war. There is sin.

Man chose to sin, and still chooses to sin every day, so man must pay sin's penalty, and the wages of sin is death. Pain, tension, trouble, disaster — all are slow forms of physical death and symbols of the spiritual death which is eternal separation from God.

What is pain? It is every sorrow the human spirit can experience consciously or unconsciously, whether understood or uncomprehended; it is the sum total of all the devastation wrought by evil from the beginning of time to the present. This is the pain from within whose deadly grip a suffering humanity cries out for answer and release.

What has the Word of God to say to the problem of human pain? Let's look into the Scriptures to find out. Whatever your personal sorrow, the comfort and strength that they offer is for you.

• 4 •

THE PERFECT PLAN

IN SEVERAL PLACES IN SCRIPTURE WE ARE GIVEN BRIEF, BRIGHT glimpses of God's sovereign plan for His creation. We are not told all we should like to know about it, but we are shown enough to give us confidence that God has, indeed, a design for His creatures, and that He is in control in His universe and will one day accomplish His purpose.

We see something of this in the first part of Paul's letter to the Ephesians (1:3-14). Here we find the three Persons of the Godhead, the Father, the Son, and the Holy Spirit, taking counsel together in the far reaches of eternity. Before the foundations of the world were laid, they met in holy convocation, and the subject of their deliberations was none other than you and I.

It is the nature of love to give itself in love, to beget. And God, whose nature is purest Love, longed to shower His love upon a family—a vast family of sons and daughters who would every one be like His glorious Son. From within the perfect and joyous intimacy that existed within the Godhead, the Eternal Father yearned to reach out in love, to create, to bless, to enrich. Love seeks an object, and the object of God's designing was the creature man.

And so, as the song says, "I was in God's mind before the world began." God came to a decision about you and me. As it is put in Romans 8:29, He "foreknew" us. Long before God created man, He had a master plan for His creation.

And God's plan was for our felicity and His glory: He willed that we should be nothing less than His children, holy as Christ is holy. "For he chose us in him before the creation of the world to be holy and blameless in His sight. In love he predestined us to be adopted as his sons through Jesus Christ, in accordance with his pleasure and will—to the praise of his glorious grace, which he has freely given us in the One he loves" (Eph. 1:4-6).

10

This is why God created mankind; *this* is His eternal purpose for you and me. And what He had willed He was well able to perform. He had the power to carry out His purpose.

But God is omniscient as well as omnipotent. Looking far into the future, God knew what would happen if He created man. Together the Holy Trinity foresaw the powers of evil seeking to seduce the creatures God would create. They saw man's fall, and the awful havoc that his sin would work not only in his own nature, but in the whole of the universe as well.

And there, in grace, long before mankind was anything but a thought in the mind of his Maker, God the Father, Son, and Holy Spirit worked out their plan for man's salvation, that God's whole purpose might be fulfilled. God, whose nature is the blazing light of perfect purity, could not tolerate the darkness of sin in His creatures. Sin would separate man eternally from his Creator. A remedy must be provided, a provision made for man's re-creation in holiness, that despite man's sin God's original purpose of sonship might be realized.

And provided it was. In the fullness of time, God Himself, in the Person of His Son, would invade man's sinful world. He would take on Himself our human nature, live a Man among men, and in His human body bear the judgment of death that His righteousness would compel Him to pronounce upon His sinful creatures.

Jesus, the God-man, would do battle with the powers of darkness and would overcome them. God would proclaim His sovereignty over death by raising Christ from the dead and exalting Him to His own right hand on the throne of the universe. He would make His resurrection power available to man in the Person of His Holy Spirit so that man, too, fallen though he was, might triumph over the powers of sin and evil. And eventually, in God's appointed hour, man should realize the fullness of his sonship and share God's glory forever in His presence, redeemed at last not only from the penalty and power of sin, but even from its very presence.

Does this not shed a ray of light and hope into the dark mystery of human suffering? God is not standing impassively by, watching evil at work in the concerns of men. He is in control, and He is working out His perfect plan for our good and His glory.

You may not understand the pain you suffer today. But if you are a Christian, you do not suffer in the dark. You have a place in God's plan. In Him is no darkness at all. One day the perfection of His design will shine forth with the radiance of noonday, and you shall realize your destiny of glory in His presence. Meanwhile, you are not alone. Your life is held in the hands of a sovereign God. In Jesus Christ you are destined for glory.

• 5 •

WHAT ABOUT EVIL?

IF GOD IS SOVEREIGN, WHY IS EVIL SO STRONG? WHERE DID EVIL come from? If God is omnipotent, why doesn't He cast evil out of His universe? No single passage in Scripture sets forth the origin of evil in straightforward, easy-to-understand terms. The Bible as a whole says very little about the matter, possibly because it has nothing to do with the story of mankind; evil was in existence long before man's creation. Nonetheless, here and there we are given a few glimpses into the subject — enough to enable us to piece together all we really need to know about it.

Throughout the Old Testament, prophecies given by God frequently had a double meaning, an ultimate meaning as well as an immediate one. Two such passages are Isaiah 14:12-15 and Ezekiel 28:11-17. The messages are directed respectively towards the king of Babylon and the prince of Tyre, but the terms used seem to be too cosmic to apply only to the persons immediately addressed. They seem ultimately to look beyond their evil objects to the forces of evil that controlled them, and thus to shed some light on the origins of evil itself.

The first passage tells of Lucifer, son of the morning, who aspired to exalt his throne above the stars of God and to be like the Most High. He was cast out of heaven into hell. The second passage describes an anointed cherub who sealed up the sum of wisdom and beauty, who was perfect in his ways until his heart was lifted up with pride in his beauty and iniquity was found in him. He, too, was cast out of the mountain of God. It is likely that these are pictures of one and the same person, called by many names in the course of Scripture, but primarily Satan, or the devil. So we have a glimpse of a superior but fallen created spirit.

We are given intimations of fallen angels as well. The book of Job, thought to be the most ancient of all Old Testament documents, mentions angels who were charged with error by God, as

13

if they had rebelled against Him (Job 4:18). The New Testament corroborates this, for Jesus speaks of everlasting fire having been prepared "for the devil and his angels" (Matt. 25:41).

Peter, in the second chapter of his second letter, told the young church that God would judge the false teachers who were troubling them just as surely as He had judged the angels who sinned, whom He did not spare, but cast down into hell and delivered into chains of darkness to be reserved unto judgment (v. 4). Jude, in verse six of his letter, also referred to God's judgment on angels who did not keep their first estate, but left their own habitation, whom God had reserved in everlasting chains under darkness unto the judgment day.

Clearly these writers believed that angels existed who had fallen from their original blessed condition and had come under God's judgment as a result. These would seem to be the demons, the followers of Satan, the "principalities and powers" against whom, Paul teaches in Ephesians 6, Christians must engage in spiritual warfare.

Thus the Holy Spirit has seen fit to give us a rudimentary if incomplete knowledge of the origin of the hierarchy of hell. Long before the creation of man, other created beings had rebelled against God in heaven, had been cast out of His presence and become His implacable enemies. Of the deep, ingrained hostility and malevolence that these evil powers feel towards God and His newer creature, man, we have plentiful Scriptural and all-too-abundant personal proof.

But there is one facet of the problem of evil on which God has shed all the light we could wish for. He has made it clear beyond question that He is sovereign in His universe. Evil may be strong, but God is stronger, and He is in control.

The Bible knows nothing of dualism, of the supposed existence of two equal powers, one good and one evil. God alone is sovereign. "I am the Lord, and there is no other; apart from me there is no God" — thus He proclaims His sovereignty (Isa. 45:5). Evil, powerful as it is — your suffering and mine — is under God's control.

But let's look more deeply into the sovereignty of God and its meaning for us today.

• 6 •

Evil: Whence and Whither?

THE FORTY-FIFTH CHAPTER OF THE PROPHECY OF ISAIAH
makes the strongest single statement about the sovereignty of God
to be found in any one passage of Scripture. We have already
quoted one verse from it: "I am the Lord, and there is no other;
apart from me there is no God."

The prophet was speaking God's Word to Cyrus II, king of
Persia. Known as Cyrus the Great, he lived about five and a half
centuries before Christ. Although Cyrus neither worshiped nor
acknowledged God, he was moved by God's sovereignty and became an instrument of good to God's captive people Israel.

God declares His reasons for this: "I will strengthen you,
though you have not acknowledged me," he tells Cyrus, "so that
from the rising of the sun, to the place of its setting men may
know there is none besides me. I am the Lord, and there is no
other" (Isa. 45:5-6). Cyrus was to become a historical demonstration
of the power of God's sovereignty.

And so, according to God's plan, the pagan Cyrus delivered
God's people from their Babylonian exile, restored the Temple at
Jerusalem at his own expense (2 Chron. 36: 22-23; Ezra 1:2, 5:13,
6:3-4; Isa. 44:28), returned its sacred vessels stolen by Nebuchad-
nezzar long before (Ezra 1:7-8, 6:5), and provided money for re-
habilitation work to take place in Judah (Ezra 3:7)—all telling
examples indeed of the power of a sovereign God.

Could not a God of such undisputed sovereignty banish evil
from His creation? Again and again our hearts turn to this question
as we ponder the "Why?" of human pain. But God does not answer
our question in this, His most comprehensive statement concerning
His sovereignty. Rather, He actually seems to complicate the
problem.

At the heart of Isaiah's prophetic word we find an astonishing
assertion. Still proclaiming His sovereignty before Cyrus, God de-

15

clares, "I form the light, and create darkness, I bring prosperity, and create disaster; I, the Lord, do all these things" (v. 7).

These words have puzzled students of the Scriptures for centuries. Can they possibly mean what they seem to say? Can God Himself actually be the author of evil? For our answer we must contemplate the character of God. We must consider it not just in the light of this one statement, but in the light of the whole of His Self-revelation.

God, who is life and light (John 1:4), who is pure and perfect love (1 John 4:8), whose name is holy (Isa. 57:15), who is of purer eyes than to behold evil (Hab. 1:13), whose very nature is light and in whom is no darkness at all (1 John 1:5), who cannot tempt any man to sin (James 1:13-14), but who gave Himself a sacrifice for our sin (Rom. 5:8-9), the God of all grace (1 Pet. 5:10) who acts in grace towards His fallen creatures to make them His very sons (Eph. 1:3-14), who is the righteous judge of all the earth (Gen. 18:25): such a God cannot possibly be the originator of evil. Yet God obviously accepts responsibility for the presence of evil in His universe.

Commenting on this verse, William Fitch points out in his book *God and Evil* (Eerdmans, 1967, p. 22), that the Hebrew word used here for *create* is *bara* — the same word as that used in Genesis when God *created* the world, *created* all living things, and *created* man in His own image.

"The word *bara* is used here, as always, when the thought of absolute creation is being considered," Fitch points out. "We may contrast it with the verbs which are used with regard to 'light' and 'peace.' 'I form the light,' 'I make peace' — that is how God speaks when light and peace are discussed. There was no need for God to 'create' either light or peace, for 'God is light, and in him is no darkness at all' [1 John 1:5], and the 'fruit of the Spirit of God is peace' [Gal. 5:22]. God shares His own life with men when He gives to them the gift of light and peace. But evil is a different thing. It requires a special creation, and so the inspired Scriptures use the word *bara* — 'I create evil.' "

Thus God asserts His sovereignty over evil. In saying that He "creates" evil, He declares His supremacy over it and so dispels forever any possibility of dualism — the existence of two equal powers, one good, one evil — in His universe.

God, then, is the Creator of evil only in the sense that when

He created first angels and then men, He gave them the gift of free will. Such a gift, which would enable His creatures freely to love and to obey Him, must of necessity have enabled them also freely to rebel against Him. The ability to "create evil" is inherent in the gift of full personhood; the free created being must have options among which to choose. It is in this sense, and in this sense only, that God may be said to have "created" evil.

Dorothy Sayers casts an oblique light on the meaning of "creating evil" in her play *The Devil To Pay* when Faustus speaks to Mephistopheles (the devil):

> FAUSTUS: Thou, Mephistopheles,
> Answer again, and this time, all the truth,
> Art thou God's henchman or His master?
> Speak!
> Who made thee?
> MEPHISTOPHELES: God, as the light makes the shadow.

In some such way, God "created" evil. But it was not God, but angels who made evil a reality in the universe; not God, but man who brought it into the world. The possibility of evil's entering the universe may be God's responsibility, but its actual presence in our midst is our own.

We humans would like to know more about the origin of evil than we do, but how could our finite minds comprehend the Infinite? God has told us all we really need to know. It is enough for us to know that He is sovereign. Enough to know that evil is under His control, that He restricts its power, that He uses it to accomplish His purposes, that one day He will eradicate it entirely from His New Creation. Enough to know the historical demonstration of His love and power in Christ's cross and resurrection. Enough to know our risen, ascended, and exalted Savior, to experience the Gift of His Holy Spirit, to rest in the certainty of His coming.

Enough to know our times are in His hand!

• 7 •

MEN — OR MARIONETTES?

Any study of the mystery of suffering must be rooted in the story of man's creation. Our first parents knew perfect felicity. Created in God's own image, in-breathed with the breath of His own life, placed in a garden planted for their pleasure by the Maker of the universe, by Him united in a marriage that was literally made in heaven, and enjoying free and joyous fellowship with the Lord God Himself — what could they have lacked? God looked out over all that He had made, and behold, it was very good. His finished creation was flawless.

We need not review the details of man's fall from this state of perfection — we know it all too well. God, creating man in His own image, had given His creatures free will. He longed for fellowship with creatures who would love and obey Him, not out of necessity, but by their own free choice. God wanted sons, not automatons; He made His creatures to be men, not marionettes.

And so God placed a single restriction on the freedom He had given. On pain of death, man was forbidden to eat of the fruit of one tree only in the garden, the Tree of the Knowledge of Good and Evil. This was to be God's testing tree.

Why would God, having seen some of His angelic creatures use His gift of free will to opt for evil and so become His enemies, later create man and give him the same gift? Who can tell? Did God make man for a higher destiny than angels? We do not know. But we do not read that God created angels in His own image, nor that He chose angels to be His adoptive sons. Neither does He seem to have provided a way of redemption for angels who fell.

Perhaps a better question might be why God created man at all when He knew beforehand of the fall that would follow. Why allow sin to enter His universe if by simply withholding the breath of life He could have prevented it?

In contemplating this question at all, we must first ask another: would we really prefer never to have been given being, never to have existed at all? A few rash souls might reply in the affirmative, perhaps, but most of us find enough value in life that even in the light of human suffering we could not. For most, then, the original question must be either irrelevant or hypocritical.

Concerning the "why" of creation, John Milton suggests in *Paradise Lost* that through man, God meant to repair the damage done by Satan to the hosts of heaven (Bk. VII, ll. 90-97, 150-61). John Stott writes (in *God's New Society*, Inter-Varsity Press, p. 39), "One answer we can tentatively give is that He destined us for a higher dignity than even creation would bestow on us. He intended to 'adopt' us, to make us the sons and daughters of His family. And in Roman law (part of the background of Paul's writing), adopted children enjoyed the same rights as natural children. The New Testament has much to say about this status of 'sonship,' its rich privileges and demanding responsibilities." And C. S. Lewis illustrates this thought by drawing the analogy of a man putting a puppy through a rigorous and painful training in order that it might transcend its natural animal destiny and rise to become a friend and companion of man (*The Problem of Pain*, Geoffrey Bles, 1940, p. 31).

We do not know God's reason for doing what He did, and we may not demand of a sovereign Creator that He explain Himself to His creatures. "How small a god that fits in the mind of a man!" an unknown writer has aptly commented. God had good and sufficient reasons for His action; we trust His sovereign wisdom and love. In full knowledge that His creatures would use His gift to reject Him rather than to obey Him, God chose to give them full personhood, including free will. God is Himself a totally free Person. How could persons created in the image of God be anything other than free?

What incredible wonder that man was made to delight the heart of the eternal God! What unspeakable loss that he should choose instead to turn to his own way! For in Adam, we all sinned. Which of us has not chosen our own will over God's will countless thousands of times? Truest definition and strongest indictment of human sin is found in Isaiah's word: "we have turned every one to his own way" (Isa. 53:6 KJV). Every one of us does it every day.

For Adam and Eve, the effect of their choice was immediate

and devastating. Until then they had known only good; then, suddenly, they were aware of evil. They knew their nakedness and sought to hide it. From being totally open, unashamed, and united, the man and his wife became self-conscious and alienated from one another.

Behind this alienation lay another and deeper one — their alienation from their Creator. No longer did they await God's coming with joy. When they heard His voice as He drew near that evening, they hid from His presence. The perfect harmony that man had enjoyed with his kind, his environment, and his God was forever broken.

Sin had separated man from his Creator. God now approached His quivering creatures in sorrow and in judgment. How could they know that He approached them in mercy as well?

• 8 •

WITH MERCY AND WITH JUDGMENT

WHEN GOD FORBADE ADAM TO EAT OF THE TREE OF KNOWL-
edge, He warned him plainly of the consequences of disobedience:
"in the day that thou eatest thereof thou shalt surely die" (Gen.
2:17 KJV).

But the serpent, in tempting Eve to disobey, craftily and
convincingly belied God's Word, declaring, "You will not surely
die" (Gen. 3:4). Eve chose to believe the Tempter and give in to
her own desires. She disobeyed God. Adam, in full knowledge of
what he was doing, added his own disobedience. And so our first
parents brought upon themselves God's judgment.

Did the guilty pair tremble in terror of immediate death as
God drew near their hiding place that fateful evening? Had they
but known it, death had already found them, for separation from
God is spiritual death, and now they were hiding from God. In
time, physical death would overtake them as well, but already
God's sentence had been carried out in the alienation they were
experiencing. God's judgment must fall upon sin.

We find it easy to think of love as being an expression of
God's nature; we do not so easily grasp the fact that anger is equally
a part of His being. Yet this is so, and it is God's wrath that calls
forth His judgment.

What is God's anger? It is His deep-seated hostility towards
evil. It is the response of His holiness towards sin, the flashing
forth of His consuming light to overthrow darkness, the action of
His righteousness against unrighteousness. It is a constant com-
ponent of His essential being which always and everywhere acts
consistently against evil.

Human anger is unpredictable. I get angry when my typewriter breaks down or the soup boils over; God is never frustrated.

21

I get impatient when I'm caught in a traffic jam because I'm in a hurry; God is never in a hurry. My anger flares because I feel threatened and am frightened; but God is neither threatened nor frightened. His anger is not like ours — volatile, capricious, unexpected. It is not malicious, vengeful, vindictive. It is directed only towards evil, and hence it is never arbitrary. How could a holy God *not* be angry at sin?

Yet the God who hates the sin never ceases to love the sinner; His mercy triumphs over judgment (James 2:12). So God spoke His mercy to His fallen creatures before He pronounced His judgment on them. He addressed Himself first to the serpent, "that ancient serpent, who is the Devil, or Satan" as he is eventually unmasked in the Apocalypse (Rev. 20:2) — condemning him to crawl forever on his belly and to eat dust, a symbol of proud Satan's ultimate humiliation and defeat. Then, He gave His promise of redemption. Still speaking to the serpent — for man's redemption and Satan's overthrow would be accomplished by a single act of mercy — He made known the perfect plan the Godhead had prepared in council together in the far reaches of eternity. He foretold the death and resurrection of the Lord Jesus Christ, that victory which would bring about the final defeat and destruction of Satan. "I will put enmity between you and the woman," He said, "and between your offspring and hers; he will crush your head, and you will strike his heel" (Gen. 3:15).

And so it came about ages later. Offspring of the woman, Son of God and Mary, Jesus Christ was "struck" by Satan when He died for the sins of the world. All the hosts of hell rejoiced as His body lay lifeless in its borrowed grave. But their victory was short-lived. The third day the Prince of Life arose, eternal Conqueror over sin and death. Satan had indeed struck the heel of the Son of God, but Christ had dealt Satan a death-blow, crushing his head beyond recovery, till in the fullness of time He will destroy him utterly.

All this was implicit in God's words to the serpent that day. This was the mercy with which God triumphed over the judgment His holiness required Him to pronounce on sinful man.

But though the decisive battle has been won, the war is not yet over. World War II was to all intents and purposes won when the Normandy beachhead was successfully established, yet fighting had to continue until Hitler was totally subdued.

In His own good time, God will eradicate all evil from His universe, and sin and Satan will be no more. Meanwhile, for His own inscrutable reasons, He allows the spiritual battle to go on, and all humanity feels its effects. But we suffer in hope, for we know that the final outcome of the conflict is assured, and Christ is Victor.

What unspeakable wonder to know that our lives are in the hands of the conquering Christ whose mercy triumphs over the judgment we deserve! What light His mercy sheds in our darkness, what comfort in our pain! Can we not safely trust ourselves to the care of our merciful Creator-Redeemer-God?

•9•

THE SHATTERED IMAGE

HAVE YOU EVER SAT BY A FOREST POOL ON A QUIET EVENING, watching the reflection of the leafy canopy mirrored in its still waters? Suddenly an acorn drops from a branch overhead. Immediately the image is shattered as wavelets circle away from the point of impact. The reflection of the leaves and branches is still visible, but it is no longer clear and lovely. Though still identifiable, the image is marred. This is what happened to God's image in man when Adam and Eve rebelled against their Creator.

And now God stood before His fallen creatures. His anger at their sin was tempered by His mercy towards His sinning but still beloved children; yet by His very nature He was compelled to pronounce judgment on them.

Among the gifts that God had given His creatures in Eden were life, sexuality, and work — three parts of man's inherent nature in the image of God. All now had come under the distortion of sin. Life had already been overtaken by death: man was alienated from God. But havoc had been wrought at every level of man's being. Henceforth while man lived, a state of enmity, total and permanent, would exist between Satan and mankind — "thy seed and her seed." Man would now be the target of all the hostility of hell, engaged in a never-ending warfare with the powers of evil. Forever man would be at war with himself, his kind, and his environment.

Sexuality, too, had been invaded by sin and pulled aside from the true. It was to this that God spoke as He addressed the woman. With what infinite sadness must He have told her of the sorrow that would now be hers in this part of life for which He had planned only joy and beauty!

In Eden, man and woman were equal. They were equal in being created by God, equal by virtue of having been made in His image, and equal in moral responsibility — each was judged for his own sin, not that of the other. They were equal in their mandate to be fruitful and multiply, and hence equal partners, though with differing roles, in marriage. And they were equal in their work — together they shared the responsibility of subduing the earth and exercising dominion over it.

Now they would suffer disharmony of the deepest kind in their sexual natures. Pain and sorrow would mar the holy and beautiful pattern God had planned. In place of mutual love and self-giving, lust and brutality would rear their ugly heads. Lust and domination had had no place in Eden, but now each partner would seek to manipulate and use the other. Now children, when they came, would bring pain and heartbreak as well as delight. The open, loving, joyous union with God and with one another that God had meant them to know had been broken; man's nature was twisted at the core. God's image in His children, maleness and femaleness together in perfect and fruitful harmony, had been shattered.

Then God turned to the man. His judgment fell on man's intrinsic need to work, for that aspect of God's image, too, had been distorted by sin. Work, an integral part of man's created nature and once a source of nothing but creativity and satisfaction, would now become unremitting toil, more often fraught with frustrations, difficulties, dangers, hardships, and hunger than with pleasure.

The ground, now cursed for man's sake, would bring forth thorns and thistles. No longer would earth produce in willing and lavish abundance. Man would now be able to wrest his food from the soil only through backbreaking labor and sweat. And, lest man should eat of the Tree of Life and so live forever in his sin, God cast him out of his garden home. He was thrust into a harsh and hostile world, a world that would now be beset by natural disasters, each working its own peculiar devastation on man's toil and livelihood.

And, in the end, death: "Dust thou art, and unto dust shalt thou return." Such is the judgment that man brought on himself by his self-will and disobedience and that he continues to engender every day he lives.

Why is there suffering in our world? Suffering entered human life when God's image in His creatures was shattered by man's sin. We do well to remember this when we ponder the "Why?" of human pain. Suffering is the inevitable result of the evil man brought into the world. We cannot blame it on God.

But God's image in man, though shattered, has not been withdrawn from His fallen creatures. Rather, God has made a way to re-create it through Jesus Christ, who is Himself "the radiance of God's glory and the exact representation of his being" (Heb. 1:3).

In Christ man may find the answer to the suffering wrought by sin. God is using this evil to form Christ's image in His new creation (Rom. 8:29; Gal. 4:19). Our pain is not forever. We suffer in hope. Through Christ, the blessings of Eden may once again be ours.

• 10 •
"EARTH FELT THE WOUND"

So saying, her rash hand in evil hour
Forth reaching to the fruit, she plucked, she eat.
Earth felt the wound, and Nature from her seat
Sighing through all her works gave signs of woe,
That all was lost. Back to the thicket slunk
The guilty serpent. . . .
  —John Milton, Paradise Lost, Book IX, ll. 780-85

THROUGHOUT THE SCRIPTURES WE FIND AN INTIMATE RELA-
tionship between God's physical and His human creation. Man's
mandate in Eden, given jointly to Adam and Eve, was to fill the
earth, to subdue it, and to have dominion over it and its creatures.
God placed Adam in the Garden "to dress it and to keep it." He
Himself brought the animals and birds to Adam to see what he
would name them, and He accepted the names Adam chose.

Man's sin had immediate repercussions throughout the physical universe: "Earth felt the wound." God had given man dominion
over the earth; when man sinned, earth, too, though innocent, was
made to share the results of his disobedience. So God told Adam
that the ground was now cursed for man's sake: no longer would
it yield him food freely; and in the end, man's body, made from
dust, must return to its earthy source.

And so we read that thorns and thistles would spring up in
the earth, and that man would eat its fruit only through sweat and
sorrow (Gen. 3:17-19). Though no other effect of man's sin is
specifically mentioned, other passages of Scripture lead us to believe
that this is but a representative allusion to the cosmic effect that
sin's entrance had on the whole of the created order.

Natural disasters — earthquakes, tornadoes, floods, volcanoes,
droughts, lightning bolts, hail and dust storms, erosion, famine,
and the like — these things that have such catastrophic effects on

27

man's welfare and food supply — were no more a part of God's original creation than were weeds, thorns, and thistles. They are part of the distortion that came with man's fall — nature out of control, as it were, with results that were never designed to be.

Was any part of the cosmos in existence before the creation of the world? We do not know. But if there were, God has not told us that it was invaded by evil because some of the angels fell. We read only that those who sinned were cast out of heaven into "the eternal fire prepared for the devil and his angels" (Matt. 25:41). When man fell, however, evil invaded the whole of the universe. Man and his world are inextricably bound up together.

There are many indications in Scripture that God's physical creation has a place in His eternal plan, and that He will eventually set it free from the bondage to death and decay that it now suffers because of man's sin. The most specific of these indications is found in Romans 8:18-23. Here all of nature is described as standing on tiptoe, eagerly awaiting the day of man's final redemption when he will attain the full glory of his sonship at Christ's return, when it, too, shall be set free. Now man and creation are groaning together as if in travail; then they shall be delivered together from the bondage to corruption they now share, and together they shall enter into the glorious liberty of the sons of God. Creation's destiny is tied into the destiny of man, both in its subjugation and in its liberation.

We do not know the form that creation's redemption will take any more than we now understand the full meaning of our own "manifestation of the sons of God." But we know that the creation, like ourselves, has a place in God's purpose, and that in some mysterious, exciting, and utterly surprising way, it, with us, is destined for glory.

Natural disasters, with their indiscriminate and calamitous effects on mankind, are not "acts of God," as we so glibly call them. Rather, they are the results of man's sin. The created order has been pulled awry. The universe as we know it bears only a shattered resemblance to the glorious cosmos that God intended it to be.

Milton was right when he wrote that earth felt the wound of man's sin. If innocent nature suffers because of man's transgression, is it so strange that man should suffer because of it? Man is responsible for the pain of the universe; man will suffer when earth convulses with the intensity of her torment.

Nor do we only share in Adam's sin; which of us has not voluntarily added his own weight of guilt to the sin of man? Together we bear the corporate responsibility for the sin and suffering to which all mankind, as well as all creation, now is heir.

Does this seem to you to be cold comfort in your sorrows? Let's look into the matter a little further. It may be a source of greater comfort than you realize.

• 11 •

THE PAIN OF THE UNIVERSE

IF WE ARE TO KNOW ANY COMFORT IN OUR SUFFERING AND find strength to bear it in a truly Christian manner, we must first set ourselves to understand it as well as is humanly possible. It is for this reason that we have spent so much time going over basic biblical principles concerning evil.

We must have a thorough grasp of what the Scriptures teach about evil, for evil is the source of all suffering. We must be quite sure in our minds that evil is no mystery to God, and that He holds all evil under His sovereign command. Evil is not a part of God's nature and did not originate with Him, but it did not come upon Him unawares, and it seems to exist by His permission. God was fully cognizant of its possibilities before He purposed man's creation. In His inscrutable power and wisdom, God uses evil, working through it to fulfill His will in ways beyond our understanding. One day, His purposes accomplished, He will eradicate all traces of evil from His universe.

Evil does not belong to man's true nature, for man was created in God's image. Evil entered our humanity from without: "an enemy did this" (Matt. 13:28). But evil has marred man's nature. This does not mean that he is incapable of any good—he still bears the image of God, however distorted. Rather, it means that no part of any of us—mind, heart, will, conscience, or anything else—remains untainted by the fall. And evil affected not only man, but the whole of creation as well: physical evil entered the universe in the wake of moral evil.

These are the realities of human existence. While we are in this life, we must live with the presence of evil and do battle with its powers. To one degree or another, all of us will be partakers in the pain of the universe. Dark and mysterious as these things may be to our finite minds, this is the teaching of the Word of God. Any consideration of human suffering must face these facts. Only

30

a solid grasp and a willing acceptance of these basic truths concerning evil can enable us to triumph in our personal war against it.

Suffering is no afterthought in human existence, but an integral part of it. Satan originated evil; God has allowed it to be; man has brought it into his universe. The wonder is not that we suffer so much, but rather that we do not suffer more than we do. None of us is without some part of life's suffering, although, of course, some suffer more than others.

Suffering viewed as a part of human life may help us in our personal struggle with pain, but it may also pose a question. If suffering is a result of God's judgment on man's sin, should we seek to alleviate it? There have been those who have opposed medical advances as being against God's will for mankind. On these grounds certain well-meaning but myopic Christians objected to Sir James Simpson's use of chloroform to assist in childbirth in the nineteenth century.

Jesus had already answered such people with the example of His life, however: He healed the sick and suffering wherever He went. Although the limited years of His ministry and the restricted geographical expanse of His travels meant that He could not hope to do more than barely touch the merest fringe of human pain, Jesus spent much of His public life ministering to human ills. He had come to earth to destroy the works of the devil (1 John 3:8); He fought evil in all its forms wherever He found them.

And although we know that suffering will never be eradicated from human life till Christ returns, we, too, should seek to destroy the works of sin, not only by easing suffering in every possible manner, but also by husbanding and restoring our ravaged earth and environment. Scientific, medical, and agricultural research are God's work. Christians must seek to better man's lot in every way—physically, morally, socially, educationally, politically, economically. God is not a sadist, and His people are not called to be masochists. We should seize every opportunity to alleviate suffering of whatever kind in every ethically responsible way we can devise.

While man's sin brought God's judgment on his intrinsic need to work, so that by his best endeavors man is unable to attain to all the good he can envisage, God still blesses the work of man's mind and hand. God's image, though marred, is still visible in His creatures, and perhaps nowhere more so than in the lofty achievements that man, despite his fallen nature, has been able to produce. Those who acknowledge God as Creator and Lord must work with all their strength for the benefit of God's creatures in every possible area of endeavor.

As long as we are in this life, however, we must share in the pain of the universe, despite our noblest efforts. How can an understanding of these things comfort and strengthen us in our own personal struggles?

• 12 •

In Understanding Be Men

THE SCRIPTURES UNEQUIVOCALLY ASSERT GOD'S SUPREMACY over the evil that man's sin has wrought in human existence. A strong belief in the sovereignty of God and His power to transmute suffering into eternal good, even glory, is the Christian's greatest weapon in his personal battle with life's calamities. How can such a certainty enable us to triumph over the violence Satan seeks to thrust upon us through our suffering? We must understand as much as we can about God's sovereignty.

First, we know that God is in control of our lives. At the heart of the universe, our sovereign God is on the throne. He reigns supreme over evil. Not only is He the Lord of the history of all mankind, He is the Lord of the individual history of each one of His children. Nothing can touch us but what His love and wisdom permit. God does not "send" our suffering in the sense that it originates with Him or that He wants us to have it; but it comes to us only with His knowledge and permission and cannot go beyond the boundary He has set for it. Evil cannot thwart God's purposes for His children; rather, He makes use of it to work out His will both for us and in us. In all things, even the evil that comes to us, God is working for His glory and our good. God is in control in His universe, and in my life and yours. We can face life's evils secure in this assurance.

Second, those who see the pain of the universe as something of which all are partakers, and who accept their personal share as being under God's control, will not be devastated when suffering overtakes them. They will see it in its true context, as part of the violence wrought by sin in the universe, but held under the sovereignty of the God they know and trust. They will be able to wage spiritual war against the evil in their suffering and to triumph over it. They will not be led off onto tangents or half-truths in the face of trouble. They will not fall prey to purveyors of questionable interpretations of miracles, healings, or deliverance.

Such Christians will fight only the evil itself — not God, not circumstances, not fear, not the accusations of conscience or, as sometimes happens, of other people. They are not tormented by self-doubt, nor by doubts concerning the power or goodness of God. They are not haunted by questions (*Why?; What if . . . ?; If God loves me, how can he do this to me?*) or reproaches (*Why didn't I . . . ?; If only!*). They do not wallow in self-pity (*Why me?; What have I done to deserve this?*). They do not fear they are experiencing God's punishment for some childhood mistake or vague, long-forgotten sin, or that somehow they have strayed outside God's will or care.

Such Christians know who they are — the children of a loving, sovereign heavenly Father. They know where they are going: they are destined for glory, and they see their trouble as part of the pain of the universe which God in mercy is using to prepare them for that destiny (Rom. 8:6-18). They trust their God to work out His purpose through their evil, and to sustain and care for them in it. They know that non-Christians also must suffer — suffer alone in the dark, unlike believers. They come to appreciate more and more deeply the resources that are theirs in Christ.

Does this mean that believers do not really suffer? Not at all. Pain is pain, and those who suffer, suffer. But there is a vast difference in our suffering. We suffer in hope (Rom. 8:20-24, 5:2) and assurance (Rom. 8:28-29). We are upheld. We know God is at work in our pain. We learn to triumph over evil even in the midst of evil, as Christ did; and the trumpet of our faith gives out no uncertain sound to those who listen. Christians who suffer conscious of the place of suffering in the will of God are able to release all their energies to fight against the evil in their situation and to overcome it.

When we learn to rest in God's sovereignty, we know great inner peace. Our pain may not grow less, our loss may not be restored, our grief may still be ours, but their power to harm us is broken. There is a vast difference between suffering in God's will and suffering apart from that assurance. No Christian need do this. God's peace of heart is ours for the taking.

When trouble strikes, we must accept it as from God, bringing it to Him and telling Him that we love and trust Him. We must claim His promise to overcome our evil with His good, and trust Him to do it in this pain. So we will work together with God to allow Him to fulfill His holy purpose for us and in us.

Practical blessings, too, come with our acceptance of God's sovereignty. When we resist our sufferings, we make life very much harder for ourselves. When we accept them and cast ourselves and our troubles on God, we suffer much less intensely.

Tension increases physical pain; dependence on God releases one from tension, and so reduces pain. Sleeplessness gives way to repose when we rest in God's love. A trusting mind thinks clearly, while a fearful one is paralyzed. Vitality, sapped by worry, heightens with confidence. Decisions are better made by minds at rest than by minds at war. Whatever our problem, knowing God's rest will make us better able to face it.

Spiritual warfare is a fierce battle at best; it takes all our spiritual strength to contend with spiritual foes. We cannot hope to triumph in such combat if we squander our forces on peripheral issues. Only by concentrating all our spiritual resources on the central issue can we hope to conquer the evil that is inherent in our suffering and so realize the good that God is working for us through it, whether in this life or in the life to come. Only strong and well-prepared Christians will succeed in learning to do this, for there are many adversaries. Trouble separates the men from the boys, whether among sufferers or those who seek to minister to them.

Friends will arrive with their diagnoses of our problem and with the best of intentions succeed in leaving us drained of all spiritual strength. Healing, deliverance, tongues, exorcism, and such demands as "Praise the Lord anyway!", "Confess your secret sin!", "You don't have enough faith!", "Get back in God's will!", "You've got to thank Him for it!" — every conceivable reason or unreason for his trouble will be heaped on the suffering Christian. All too few, alas, will be those friends or counselors who are able to get to the heart of the matter and minister with true grace and comfort. Only those who have had to undergo such devastating experiences can know how sadly true this is. Let us strive for maturity and understanding in our dealings with suffering!

"God is sovereign in my life. God is working for my good, *even in this*": this is the certainty and comfort that God means us to have. Only a firm grasp of this truth and a willingness to accept our part in the pain of the universe rather than to waste our energies in resisting it can bring comfort and strength in our suffering and enable us to present an adequate confession of our faith to a questioning world of anguished watchers.

• 13 •

OCCUPIED TERRITORY

THE OLDER I GROW, THE MORE SIGNIFICANCE I SEE IN THE
first three chapters of Genesis. They shed more light on the im-
ponderables of life than anything else I know. Here is both the
cause of our human predicament and its cure, the source of all the
sorrows that beset us and the promise of our redemption and
ultimate triumph over evil. The truth is that we are living in
occupied territory. Our universe is occupied against its will by
powerful enemy forces.

During World War II, thousands of people had to witness
their countries overrun by alien troops, had to submit, however
unwillingly, to foreign rule. Yet in most of these countries strong
resistance movements sprang into life. Though living under enemy
rule, large numbers of loyal citizens banded together secretly, often
at risk of their lives, to find ways of outwitting the invaders. They
sabotaged the enemy's efforts and hindered his military advances,
thus furthering their own cause and speeding their own liberation.

Our present situation is something like this. Though we are
subjects of the King of kings and citizens of heaven, we live in a
universe where rebel forces of evil have real and powerful authority.

For His own inscrutable reasons, the Lord of the universe
has allowed these enemy invaders temporary residence and powers
in His dominion. Having Himself given the free will by which man
welcomed alien forces into his world, God could not summarily
cast out the intruders without negating that gift, violating man's
personality and robbing him of his dignity. Who could respect a
God who would bestow a gift, then take it back when it was used
contrary to His hopes? The eternal Father had a higher view of
man than to do that.

No, the spiritual warfare man introduced must be carried to
its conclusion. God created man in order to adopt him into His
own family and make him like Jesus Christ. Man's sin shattered

God's image in His creation; in response God set about the long, slow process of re-creating that image by redeeming His creatures through Christ and perfecting them through the working of His Holy Spirit. And God displays His sovereignty over evil by using the very suffering that is inherent in evil to assist in the working out of His eternal purpose. In the fullness of time His redeemed family, like white lilies arisen pure and fragrant from an open sewer or compost heap, shall show forth the holy radiance of Christ's image in His presence forever.

The battle has been joined and must proceed. But unlike the wartime armies of occupation whose authority was virtually absolute once they had overrun a country, the powers of evil in the universe have been given strong but clearly defined and limited authority which they exercise only under God's sovereign control. Like resistance fighters in occupied territory, Christians seek to strike back against Satan and hinder his progress and rule. At every turn as we do so, we encounter all the hostility of hell.

Yet in reality our adversaries are themselves citizens of a conquered realm and a defeated prince. They know that when the Lord of the universe speaks His ultimate Word, we, their unwilling temporary subjects, will be liberated and they themselves doomed to join their rebel leader in outer darkness. While they may, they use every power at their disposal to harass the subjects of the Prince of Life and to further the cause of their own Prince of Darkness.

Milton depicts this invisible warfare with larger-than-life reality in his *Paradise Lost.* He envisages Satan and his followers tormented in hell, consumed by their rage and hatred of the God who had cast them out of heaven, and seeking revenge. Hearing rumor of God's new world and of man, His new creature, they see their opportunity. If only they can invade this new territory and subjugate man, they can strike back, in some measure at least, against their mighty conqueror. After much effort they succeed, bringing about the fall of man. "Earth felt the wound" in that hour, and her agony continues to this day.

Milton's poem portrays a deep and important truth. Satan torments mankind to the limits of his power today in an effort to avenge himself on his conqueror. He knows he is a defeated foe with limited tenure and power. He has not forgotten the edict of Genesis and the victory of Calvary. He knows his time is running

out. In fury and desperation he hurls his every fiendish energy
against God's people, seeking through their hurt to destroy some
small part of God's kingdom.

John Bunyan vividly portrays our spiritual warfare in his
allegory *Pilgrim's Progress.* The hero of the tale, Christian, flees the
Kingdom of Darkness to the Celestial City and is beset by Satan's
devices at every turn. At one juncture, Apollyon confronts Christian, determined to destroy him in hand-to-hand combat. He shrieks
his defiance of God: "I am an enemy to this Prince; I hate His
person, His laws, and people; I am come out on purpose to withstand thee. . . . Prepare theyself to die; for I swear by my infernal
den, that thou shalt go no farther: here will I spill thy soul."

The battle that ensues is all too familiar in Christian experience. It is the kind of hostility we Christians must encounter
while we live in occupied territory.

Why do the righteous suffer? All humanity must share in
the pain of the universe, and Christians are no exception. God has
never promised His children immunity to the evils that are common to fallen man. Even the righteous will know their portion of
such suffering. And in addition, Christians will experience special
attacks as Satan comes out on purpose to withstand those who are
in any way resistance fighters for the kingdom of God. "Here will
I spill thy soul" is no idle threat. Satan will never cease trying to
incapacitate God's resistance fighters; more than one Christian has
already fallen before the onslaughts of Apollyon. Only the sword
of the Spirit — the Word of God clearly understood and well used —
can enable us to withstand Satan's attacks and remain victors on
the field.

• 14 •
THE ENEMY

SINCE WE MUST DO BATTLE WITH THE POWERS OF DARKNESS, we must learn all we can about our Adversary and his tactics. The Christian church today lacks solid teaching on the subject of Satan. Some Christians take the existence of the powers of darkness so seriously that they see even the most commonplace happenings of daily experience in terms of demons; others live as if Satan and his evil hosts did not exist. The devil is never happier than when he sees us hold one extreme position or the other. We need a balanced biblical view of the reality of our foe if we are to triumph over the evil Satan seeks to work in our hearts and lives.

We see plenty of evidence of the works of Satan in the Old Testament, but we are told little of his person. In the New Testament, however, we learn much about the devil. Jesus Himself is the source of most of our information, and Paul and other apostolic writers corroborate and expand His teaching.

Jesus' knowledge of Satan is thorough and reliable. In His pre-incarnate existence Jesus had first-hand experience of Satan's creation, saw his fall, and witnessed his seduction of mankind. He Himself came to earth "to destroy the devil's work" (1 John 3:8; Heb. 2:14-15). He experienced the devil's temptation in the wilderness and overcame him (Matt. 4:4-11). He was "struck" by Satan when He gave His life for our sins on the cross, but He dealt him a mortal wound ("crushed his head") when He rose from the dead. Now the Lord Jesus is exalted at God's right hand, sovereign over all evil. One day He will banish sin and Satan from His universe.

The Hebrew name for the devil, *Satan,* means "Adversary"; its Greek equivalent means "Slanderer." Always Satan is the Adversary of our souls. But in the Scriptures he is called by other names as well.

He is "the evil one" (Matt. 13:19, 38), "the enemy ... the devil" (Matt. 13:39). He "was a murderer from the beginning, not holding to the truth, for there is no truth in him"; he is "a liar and the father of lies" (John 8:44).

He is "Beelzebub, the prince of demons" (Matt. 12:24); "the ruler of the kingdom of the air, the spirit who is now at work in those who are disobedient" (Eph. 2:2); "the prince of this world" who shall be judged and cast out (John 12:31). He is "the god of this age [who] has blinded the minds of unbelievers" (2 Cor. 4:4). He is the "great dragon . . . that ancient serpent called the devil or Satan" (Rev. 12:9). He is "the tempter" (Matt. 4:3).

He is "your enemy the devil [who] prowls around like a roaring lion looking for someone to devour" (1 Pet. 5:8). He is "the accuser" of God's people (Rev. 12:10) who "has sinned from the beginning" (1 John 3:8) and who "leads the whole world astray" (Rev. 12:9). He "holds the power of death" (Heb. 2:14), and hence is "the last enemy" that shall be destroyed (1 Cor. 15:26).

Satan has his schemes (Eph. 6:11; 2 Cor. 2:11) and his traps (1 Tim. 3:7; 2 Tim. 2:26). He deceives with cunning (2 Cor. 11:3), leads astray (Rev. 12:9), torments (2 Cor. 12:7), tempts (1 Thess. 3:5), pursues (Rev. 12:13), and blasphemes (Rev. 13:6).

Satan is allowed to test God's people, and among those he has tested are Job (Job 1:6-12, 2:1-6) and Paul (2 Cor. 12:7-10). He works through people — some of them even God's people, such as Judas (John 13:27), Ananias and Sapphira (Acts 5:3), and Peter (Luke 22:31; Matt. 16:23). He infiltrates God's people with his own "sons" in order to hinder God's work (Matt. 13:38). He can cause physical disabilities, as in the case of the woman who was crippled by a spirit, whom Jesus healed one Sabbath day (Luke 13:10-17).

Satan is always and everywhere in conflict with good, seeking not only to corrupt men (Luke 22:31), but even archangels (Jude 9); and resisting and accusing God's people even in His very presence (Job 1:9; Zech. 3:1-2; Rev. 12:10). He is constantly working against the best interests of mankind, particularly God's people. And he is aided in his evil designs by a host of "principalities and powers" to whom we turn in our next chapter.

With such an Adversary, can we wonder that suffering is a part of human life?

• 15 •

PRINCIPALITIES AND POWERS

AT THE OUTSET OF WORLD WAR I, BRITISH TROOPS EMBARKED for France blithely singing silly war ditties, and assuring one another that the war would be over in a few weeks and they'd all be home for Christmas. That Christmas was a long time coming. They had no idea of the strength, the numbers, or the commitment of the enemy they had set out to fight. We, too, must take note of the resources, the malevolence, and the might of our enemy if we are not to go down to defeat in the spiritual warfare in which every true Christian must be engaged.

Satan does not carry on his evil work unaided. Behind him are his back-up forces, the hosts of fallen angels who joined him in his rebellion against God and were cast out of heaven with him to become part of the hierarchy of hell. Paul refers to them as "the principalities and powers in heavenly places" (Eph. 3:10 KJV), "the powers of this dark world ... the spiritual forces of evil in the heavenly realms" (Eph. 6:12).

Principalities and powers, then, are powerful and demonic cosmic intelligences working under the control and command of Satan. Their realm of operations is "the heavenly places," which John Stott defines as "the unseen world of spiritual reality" (*God's New Society,* Inter-Varsity Press, p. 81). And these are the same "heavenly places" where the exalted Savior now sits at the right hand of God, and to which Paul teaches that we, too, as members of God's family, have been raised and seated with Him (Eph. 1:19-22, 2:4-7).

Small wonder, then, that Christians experience spiritual warfare! We live in a battlefield. Yet in that unseen world of spiritual reality, our God is sovereign. The conqueror of Calvary is on the throne. He means His people to share His victory in their individual struggles against the powers of evil. Let's gather together the biblical teachings concerning principalities and powers. It is surprising how much information we are given.

Like Satan himself, principalities and powers were created by God, and subsequently fell: "by him all things were created: things in heaven and on earth, visible and invisible, whether thrones or powers or rulers or authorities; all things were created by him and for him" (Col. 1:16).

The Scriptures do not specifically tell us of their fall, but since part of Christ's work was to subdue them, we know that they were in rebellion against God. Paul describes the magnitude of Christ's victory over them: "having spoiled principalities and powers, he made a shew of them openly, triumphing over them in it" (Col. 2:15 KJV). He also states that God raised Christ from the dead by His mighty power and "set him at his own right hand in the heavenly places, far above all principality, and power, and might, and dominion, and every name that is named, not only in this world, but also in that which is to come: And hath put all things under his feet" (Eph. 1:20-22 KJV).

Peter tells us that Jesus Christ "has gone into heaven and is at God's right hand — with angels, authorities and powers in submission to him" (1 Pet. 3:22). And Paul declares that he is persuaded that "neither death, nor life, nor angels, nor principalities, nor powers, nor things present, nor things to come, nor height, nor depth, nor any other creature, shall be able to separate us from the love of God, which is in Christ Jesus our Lord" (Rom. 8:38-39 KJV). Certainly the principalities and powers have been totally defeated by Jesus Christ.

Part of God's purpose for His church is to demonstrate to the principalities and powers in heavenly places through His redeemed family His own "manifold wisdom" (Eph. 3:9-11). In full view of all His creation, God will make a public display of His wisdom "in all its varied forms" (Eph. 3:10 NEB), "the complex wisdom of God's plan being worked out through the Church, in conformity to that timeless purpose which he centered in Christ Jesus, our Lord" (Eph. 3:11 JBP). Through His many-tongued, many-cultured, many-colored, and multinational church, God will proclaim before His enemies the wisdom and power of their Creator.

The principalities and powers are the implacable enemies of God and His people. They are servants of the Prince of Darkness, and like him they are both wicked and cunning. Against these evil powers the Christian must constantly do battle. For this warfare, God has provided spiritual armor: "For we wrestle not against flesh and blood, but against principalities, against powers, against the rulers of the darkness of this world, against spiritual wickedness in high places. Wherefore take unto you the whole armor of God" (Eph. 6:12-13 KJV)

But hostile and powerful as they are, the principalities and powers will one day be totally destroyed. Like their evil master, they are a conquered foe; they share the death-wound that Satan received at Calvary. Their powers, though strong, are both temporary and limited. When Christ returns to consummate His conquest, He will put away all evil forever: "the end will come, when he hands over the kingdom to God the Father after he has destroyed all dominion, authority and power. For he must reign until he has put all his enemies under his feet" (1 Cor. 15:24-25).

Meanwhile, the spiritual warfare rages, and we are all involved. The principalities and powers, skilled subjects of their wicked master, employ his tactics as they seek to render God's people powerless in His service. What are these tactics, and how may we learn to triumph over them?

• 16 •

TEMPTER-DECEIVER-ACCUSER-DEVOURER

SATAN HAS MANY STRATAGEMS FOR HARMING GOD'S PEOPLE. Four of the most dangerous are expressions of his malevolent personality. Let's look at them.

First, Satan is the *Tempter*. He tempts us today in the same way he tempted Eve and sought to tempt Christ —by appealing to our natural desires, what 1 John 2:16 calls "the cravings of sinful man, the lust of his eyes and the boasting of what he has and does." When Eve saw that the forbidden fruit was good for food, pleasant to look at, and able to make her wise, she disregarded God's command and reached out for it (Gen. 3:6). We are all too easily tempted today to gratify our appetites in similar ways. Satan and his minions daily offer us a bewitching array of fascinating and deceptive enticements.

Second, Satan is the *Deceiver*. His consummate skill in this role is possibly the greatest single reason we so often fall into temptation; he seldom tempts overtly. It was "the serpent's cunning" that deceived Eve (2 Cor. 11:3), and he approaches us in the same way. The Scriptures warn us to be wary of "the devil's schemes" (Eph. 6:11) and traps (1 Tim. 3:7; 2 Tim. 2:26) and of the stratagems by which he seeks to outwit us (2 Cor. 2:11).

There is no truth in Satan. He is a liar and the Father of Lies (John 8:44) who deceives the nations (Rev. 20:3) and leads the whole world astray (Rev. 12:9). He will never cease trying to deceive us; and he succeeds, alas, all too often.

Satan can and does transform himself into "an angel of light" (2 Cor. 11:14) in practicing his deceptions. By his "false Christs and false prophets," and the false "signs and miracles" he enables them to perform, he deceives God's people, seeking to deceive "even the elect" (Matt. 24:24). He does, indeed, "seduce" some

44

believers (1 John 2:26 KJV). In his parable of the tares (Matt. 13:38-42), Christ warns that the weeds Satan has sown will be indistinguishable from the wheat until the harvest. Meanwhile, the tares, his "sons," exist often unrecognized in our churches, sometimes even in positions of leadership.

Satan may indeed roar like a lion (1 Pet. 5:8), but he is more likely to approach us in one of his gentler guises, seeking to deceive us into accepting his false teachers, false standards and goals, and false doctrines. He attempts to beguile us into trying to do God's work using his methods. He will seek to darken our minds, cloud our judgment, weaken our faith, lure us off onto tangents, or undermine our belief in the Scriptures — "Yea, hath God said . . . ?" (Gen. 3:1 KJV). He will even lull us into thinking that he does not exist. He will do anything and everything to hinder God's work in us and through us. He is the Arch-Deceiver.

Third, Satan is the *Accuser,* who accuses God's people before Him day and night (Rev. 12:10). Strange that he should continue to accuse us before God in face of the victory of Calvary, but this is what the Scriptures tell us he does. These accusations, however, cannot harm us. They are answered on our behalf by our advocate there, Jesus, our great high priest, who is now appearing in the presence of God for us (Heb. 9:24) — the exalted Christ Himself.

But Satan has another form of accusation with which he can and all too frequently does shackle God's people. He accuses our conscience and saddles our spirits with false guilt. Thus he effectively paralyzes our usefulness to God.

When we confess a sin, repenting of it and forsaking it, God forgives us and purifies us from all unrighteousness (1 John 1:9). Such sin can accuse us no more; it has no more power over us. God forgets it and so must we — except to remember to avoid it in future. Christians live every day under the forgiveness of God.

Satan, however, works on our conscience with memories of past sins, burdening us with feelings of uncertainty, failure, hopelessness, unworthiness, remorse, even despair. How well he knows that as long as he can keep us occupied with introspection and self-accusation, he renders us powerless in spiritual warfare against evil!

Satan seeks to burden us with a load of guilt from which there seems to be no escape; the Holy Spirit, on the other hand, convicts us of sin in our lives — usually specific sin in contrast to Satan's vague generalities — and then leads us to repentance, confession, and forgiveness. We must learn to differentiate between the two voices and respond accordingly, rebuking the Accuser and acting on the promptings of the Holy Spirit.

Fourth, Satan is the *Devourer*. The Scriptures warn us that "your enemy the devil prowls around like a roaring lion looking for someone to devour" (1 Pet. 5:8). In this capacity, Satan seeks not to tempt the believer into sin, to deceive him into error, or to accuse him into spiritual paralysis, but physically to incapacitate or even to kill him, so great is his hostility towards God and His kingdom.

In Revelation 12:3-4 we read that the "enormous red dragon [Satan] . . . stood in front of the woman [Israel] . . . so that he might devour her child [Jesus] the moment it was born." In Matthew 2:16 we note that Satan moved Herod to try to accomplish this by what we call "the slaughter of the innocents" when he heard of Jesus' birth.

Satan still seeks to devour God's people, and on occasion he succeeds, though only under the sovereignty of God. Some, though not all illnesses among Christians, and some, though not all premature deaths may be the work of the Devourer. On other occasions it is likely that God has fulfilled His promise of Malachi 3:11 (KJV)—"I will rebuke the devourer for your sakes"—and withheld Satan from succeeding in his nefarious design.

Even if he is allowed to devour a believer, Satan's triumph must turn to ashes in his mouth, for he is unable to prevent the Holy Spirit from multiplying the influence of the Christian's life as He has done with martyrs from earliest times into the present. By his very malevolence, Satan urges his victim into God's immediate presence, making possible the accomplishment of God's highest purpose of "glorifying" man—perfecting in him the image of Christ whom he now sees face to face (1 John 3:2).

One summer I had a personal experience both of Satan as Devourer and of God as sovereign Deliverer in connection with the writing of this book. For some years I had been under constraint to write something on the meaning of suffering but had been unable to get down to it. Finally I had been able to set aside three months in which to give myself entirely to ordering my thoughts on the subject and committing them to paper.

On the last Saturday in May, I set out by myself to drive to the wilderness retreat where I hoped to write without interruption through the summer. I noted that while traffic was light going north on the superhighway, it was very heavy going south to the city — an unusual situation indeed for a summer weekend. It was raining lightly but steadily. I experienced no problems in piloting my car, which was heavily loaded with typewriter, books, cat, food for three months, and other assorted necessities, on towards my lovely island home.

For the first hour or so I traveled on a divided highway, but as I was approaching the spot at which the two streams merged into a single four-lane highway, a car pulled from a roadside flea market onto the road in front of me, cutting me off. I had to brake suddenly and change lanes to avoid hitting it. I went into a skid on the wet pavement.

My car slid out of control into the southbound lanes, executed two mad figure eights in the midst of the heavy traffic, spun into a pile of construction sand heaped along the edge of the road, and was flung backwards towards the ditch. I felt the car's back wheels drop and knew it was flipping over, rear first. Simultaneously my front wheels sank into sand, stopping the engine. Looking shakily out, I saw that I had a bare toehold in the sand, enough for my trembling feet to grasp gingerly as I eased myself through the driver's door. There I saw the rest of the car hanging precariously over a fourteen-foot abyss.

As I stood there afraid even to lean against the hood, I was conscious of only one thing: Satan had tried to kill me, but God had delivered me out of his hand. I knew with certainty that I had been spared for one purpose — to write a book that Satan obviously did not want written, since it would seek to unmask him for the evil power that he is. Stronger than my emotional shock or the trauma of what had so nearly happened was my sense of compulsion to triumph in this piece of spiritual warfare apportioned me by God, to seek to further the work of His kingdom and discomfit His enemies. Within half an hour of so close a brush with death, I was back on the road, driving on to my isolated cabin and the task that awaited me. Neither the car nor I had suffered a scratch. So great is the sovereign power of the living God.

Tempter, Deceiver, Accuser, Devourer — how can we hope to overcome this powerful Adversary? God has given us guidelines to follow. Let's find out what they are.

• 17 •

SPIRITUAL STRATEGY

GOD'S GUIDELINES TO VICTORY OVER OUR SPIRITUAL ENEMIES
are scattered throughout Scripture. Pieced together, they tell us all
we need to know — though I frankly admit that it is easier to write
about spiritual strategy than to put it into practice. Let's look at
five biblical guidelines for overcoming the Adversary.

First, we must know and use the Word of God. When Jesus
was tempted by Satan following His baptism (Matt. 4:1-11), He
turned back the devil's thrusts with a single statement: "It is written." He replied to each temptation with a scriptural quotation
against which the Tempter could make no answer. On one occasion
Satan tried to deceive Jesus by making a counter-quotation which
he took out of context from Psalm 91, but Jesus was not deceived —
He knew the Scriptures thoroughly. Following the Lord's third
scriptural assault on His foe, the devil left Him.

No matter what guise Satan may approach us in, the Word
of God will always be our strongest weapon against him: "the
sword of the Spirit . . . is the word of God" (Eph. 6:17). But if we
are to use the Scriptures to advantage, we must first be thoroughly
familiar with them. We must hide God's Word in our minds and
hearts. We must know its meaning, its context, its applicability to
our situation. We must know how to use it. An unknown and
untried sword is useless in the kind of hand-to-hand combat that
we must do with our wily foe.

Second, we must put on the whole armor that God has
provided for our protection. If we are to triumph over the enemy,
we must not only be aware of God's armor, but deliberately put
it on and learn to use it (Eph. 6:10-18; 1 Thess. 5:8). Our strength
for combat is in God alone; only as we actively and purposefully
draw on His strength will we be able to use His weapons. We must
know our foes — their power, their cunning, their wickedness. We

must believe that God's strength and provision is sufficient to make us able to stand against them.

Paul outlines God's all-encompassing provision for His people in his letter to the Ephesians. Here Paul tells us that we must buckle on God's girdle of truth — His eternal truth and our own acceptance of the demands that such truth makes on our lives: only transparently truthful people can use God's armor. In addition, we must put on the breastplate of righteousness, Christ's righteousness, which He has imparted to us, along with our own active and purposeful desire to live holy and righteous lives. Our feet must be shod with God's offer of peace through the Gospel of Jesus Christ — no other message will do — and we must be His peace-makers in our daily lives. We must hold high the shield of faith — our total belief in God and in His Word, against which all Satan's fiery darts are helpless. We must wear the helmet of salvation — stand fast in the certainty that God has already saved us from sin's penalty, that He is saving us even now from its power, and that He will one day save us forever even from its very presence. Faith is sufficient for the present, and hope for the future. Both are encircled by God's unchanging love. We must possess and use the Spirit's sword, the Word of God, and we must cover all our endeavor with fervent and unceasing prayer, for we are dependent on the Spirit of God alone for our victory.

Third, we must be alert and watchful at all times. The best of weapons are useless to soldiers who relax their vigilance. We must be careful that we give Satan no opportunity to gain an advantage over us. Paul teaches this when he speaks about righteous anger in Ephesians 4:26-27: " 'In your anger do not sin,' " he tells us. "Do not let the sun go down while you are still angry, and do not give the devil a foothold." Satan is always ready and waiting to catch us at an off moment — as, for example, when he urges us to unholy anger in the wake of righteous anger that we have somehow allowed to linger overlong. For the same reason, Peter warns us to "be self-controlled and alert," lest Satan get an advantage over us (1 Pet. 5:8). Jesus warned His disciples many times to be watchful, alert, ready. A sober recognition of the possibility of danger, and vigilance that we allow Satan no opportunity to gain the ascendency over us at any time — these must be our watchwords if we would be victorious in the battle with our crafty assailant.

Fourth, we must resist our Adversary. Not only do the Scriptures exhort us to submit ourselves to God, they teach that we must actively resist Satan: "Resist the devil, and he will flee from you" (James 4:7). "Resist him, standing firm in the faith," urges Peter (1 Pet. 5:9). Paul teaches that God's armor is given in order that we may stand our ground against Satan, and having done that, may remain victors on the field. Again, he urges us to "fight the good fight of the faith" (1 Tim. 6:12). We are to carry the fight into the enemy's territory, drive back the Usurper, and win new ground for the kingdom of God.

We do this by fleeing from temptation (1 Cor. 6:18, 10:14; 2 Tim. 6:11, 2:22) and resisting Satan. When the Tempter points us to something alluring which is in reality a trap into which he wishes to entice us, we must turn and flee from the prospect, no matter how appealing or rational it may seem. In so doing we face our Adversary in the name of our God and resist him in hand-to-hand combat.

And finally, in all our strategy, we rely on the help of the Holy Spirit and call on Him for aid. Only He can teach us how to put on the heavenly armor and to wield His sword. Only He can communicate to us the secrets of vigilance, resistance, attack, and flight from temptation. "When the enemy shall come in like a flood, the Spirit of the Lord shall lift up a standard against him" (Isa. 59:19 KJV). We must call on Him to lead us in using the strategies by which the Scriptures instruct us to overcome our wicked Antagonist and his demonic followers and fight beneath His conquering banner.

During World War II, the Battle of Britain was fought and won in the air over Europe as British fliers defended their homeland against Hitler's planned invasion. The one hope of the defense pilots was to gain enough altitude to come upon the enemy planes from above and fight downwards.

Our spiritual warfare, too, takes place in high places. We wrestle not against flesh and blood, but against principalities and powers, against the rulers of the darkness of this world, against spiritual wickedness "in the heavenly realms" — the invisible sphere of spiritual reality (Eph. 6:12). Like the wartime fighter pilots, our only hope is to attack our adversaries from above. We must fight from a position higher than theirs if we are to triumph.

And is not this just what God has planned for His children? He raised Christ from the dead and set Him at His own right

hand, far above all principalities and powers and might and dominion and every name that is named, both in this world and that
which is to come, and has put all things under His feet (Eph.
1:20-22). In Christ we have instant altitude above our every foe.
By faith we may share Christ's victory, may fight against our deadly
enemies, and may overcome.

What has all this to do with human suffering? Let's see how
it works out in practical experience now!

• 18 •

WHEN TROUBLE STRIKES

DOES IT SEEM TO YOU THAT WE HAVE STRAYED AWAY FROM our original topic in these past few chapters? I assure you that we have not digressed. Integral to any consideration of the problem of human suffering is a thorough knowledge of Satan and his tactics and a firm grasp of God's mighty defenses against his evil designs.

Much of our hope of learning to triumph over the sorrows that invade our lives lies in our understanding their origin and nature. Until we know what the Scriptures teach about evil, we are likely to fall prey to Satan's wiles when trouble strikes. Time and effort devoted to tracing God's design is wisely spent, for in this way we can build a solid base from which to operate in time of need.

We must never underestimate the wickedness, power, or cunning of our Adversary. To do so is to go down to certain defeat before him. But though we must know and respect our enemy, we need not fear him. The goodness and the greatness of God far exceed Satan's limited though very real powers. Like the lions blocking Christian's path to the Palace Beautiful in *Pilgrim's Progress,* the devil is chained. God holds the chains, some shorter, some longer, in His sovereign control. Satan can go so far in his evil purposes against us, but no farther. Christians do well to think deeply on these truths.

All human suffering originates in Satan. Its nature, like his, is only and always evil. By afflicting God's people, Satan seeks to keep them from enjoying the benefits of God's mercy and to render them powerless in the spiritual struggle in order to hinder the advance of God's kingdom. He will stop at nothing to achieve his nefarious goal.

When suffering befalls us, whether physical illness, devastating circumstance, or some other form of human pain, we must look it in the face and assess it. We must ask ourselves some penetrating questions about it. Only the Scriptures can give us the answers we need.

Satan is the originator of our trouble, but God has allowed it to come into our lives. Satan is seeking to work us harm through it, but God has promised to work through all things, even this, for our ultimate good and His glory. What should be our attitude towards our suffering?

First, contrary to belief popular in some Christian circles today, we do not have to thank God for our pain. To do so would be to thank Him for evil, and thus, in the last analysis, for sin. God abominates both sin and evil; to thank Him for them is to imply that they originated with Him. If we think we must thank God for the suffering that results from sin, we display a woeful ignorance of the nature of God. God is no sadist, tormenting His creatures and requiring them to praise Him for their torment. He suffers in our sorrows more deeply than we do, for He knows, as we cannot, the perfection of His design for mankind and the distortion wrought in it by man's sin.

No, we ought not thank God for our affliction. But we should thank Him, and robustly, for the sovereign love, wisdom, and power with which He will overrule our seemingly evil circumstances to work eternal good for us through them. We must praise Him for His promises and rest our souls upon His sovereign truth. In Jesus' name we must reject all that is of Satan in our suffering, trusting God to restrain his power and overcome the evil. Then we can set about doing what we can to withstand Satan and to triumph over the harm he seeks to work us in our trouble.

What does it mean to "rebuke Satan"? The phrase is common among Christians today. It seems to have a variety of connotations, not all of which are truly biblical. To many it means a verbal formula — almost an incantation supposedly having semi-magical powers against the Evil One. A Christian psychiatrist once told me of a patient of his who began every day by rebuking Satan. By this he meant that she addressed certain words to Satan that were supposed to stay his power against her. She was troubled that despite her having said the correct words, her days were full of problems and failure.

Only once in the Gospels do we read that Jesus "rebuked the devil" (in Matt. 17:18 KJV). The marginal reading there uses the word *demon* rather than *devil,* and the newer translations use *demon* exclusively. I have been unable to find any biblical instance in which a person is said to have rebuked Satan, although in a few places we read of God doing so. Lacking a clear biblical example, I am not sure that Christians have any mandate to rebuke Satan; in any case, no mantra-like words will enable us to do so.

On the other hand, Satan is rebuked when we follow the biblical principles of faith and obedience towards our sovereign God. We rebuke Satan, in effect, when in defiance of the evil he seeks to work us, we affirm our confidence in God's power and goodness; when, despite our painful circumstances, we resist his attempts to take our eyes off Christ; when, notwithstanding our suffering, we refuse to give way to self-pity, fear, or unbelief.

It is in the biblical way of rebuking Satan that our knowledge of his devices will stand us in good stead. We must watch vigilantly that in our pain and upset we do not allow Satan to get an advantage over us. We must resolutely refuse to listen to the voice of the Tempter and give in to fear, worry, self-pity, or despair. We must repudiate the Accuser as he seeks to burden our conscience with sins God has long ago forgiven and forgotten. We must call the Deceiver by his ugly name when he whispers lies about God's love, power, or sufficiency, hurling him back with the Word of God as Jesus did. We must defy the Devourer, knowing that God is Lord of life and death, and that to be absent from the body is to be present with the Lord. We must resist the devil night and day, bombarding him with God's promises and voicing over and over again our unassailable belief in God's sovereignty.

We must take our stand on the whole Word of God, not just on some parts of it. In our hearts and minds we must trace and retrace its teaching concerning the overarching design of God's eternal plan, and deliberately place ourselves and our suffering within the perfect circle of His sovereign love and power. We must ask God to use our trouble to draw us closer to Himself, and to teach us how to make use of our suffering for spiritual growth and wholeness. We must trust Him to work through it to form in us ever more clearly the holy image of Jesus Christ, which is God's highest purpose for His children and our highest good and ultimate glory.

Because we are still fallen creatures even though we are Christians, we can hinder God from working out His purposes through the evil that comes to us, and sometimes, alas, we do. What tragedy to suffer and to harvest only loss rather than the spiritual gain that God longs to give us! Nothing can please our Adversary more.

We may indeed suffer pain and sorrow, but we need not suffer loss. We must actively cooperate with God, however, if we are to rob the Evil One of his spoil in the arena of suffering. Our strongest weapon is a thorough knowledge of the whole counsel of God. Let us not fail to use it to learn to triumph over Satan, that we may miss nothing of the glory for which God has destined us in Christ Jesus, and for which He is even now preparing us.

• 19 •

"THERE WAS A DAY"

HOW CAN WE BE CERTAIN THAT OUR SUFFERING IS HELD IN the sovereign hand of God? What a human question this is! The Word of God teaches God's sovereignty over the affairs of men in many places, but never more vividly and compellingly than in the book of Job.

Job was a wealthy patriarch and herdsman who lived in the land of Uz long ago. Father of seven sons and three daughters, he was master of a large and prosperous household, a man of substance, the greatest of all the men of the east. He feared God and shunned evil and taught his family to do the same, even rising early in the morning to offer sacrifices on their behalf lest any of them should unwittingly have transgressed the law of God. He was so upright that God Himself called him "a perfect . . . man" (Job 1:8 KJV).

The Scriptures tell us that "there was a day" when there was a convocation in heaven. The sons of God came to present themselves before the Lord, and for some reason Satan presented himself among them. God asked Satan if he had considered the uprightness of His servant Job. Satan challenged God, contending that Job's godliness was contingent upon the prosperity God had given him. God responded to Satan's charge by allowing him to impoverish Job utterly, excepting only his person.

Satan got busy. One calamity after another descended on poor Job. With devastating swiftness his livelihood, servants, flocks, herds, and even his ten children were swept away. Job's response to his catastrophe was one of sublime faith: "The Lord gave, and the Lord has taken away; may the name of the Lord be praised" (Job 1:21).

Again "there was a day" when there was a convocation in heaven. Again Satan presented himself among the sons of God. God pointed out Job's continuing godliness despite his overwhelming, undeserved, and unexplained suffering. Again Satan challenged God. Let harm come to Job's person, he argued, and his integrity would crumble. This time God gave Satan permission to afflict Job's body, reserving only his life from Satan's power.

Satan went into action again. This time he caused Job to break out in boils from head to foot. His wife, faithful to her husband in his first affliction, turned on him now, urging him to curse God and die. After being a highly honored man of distinction, almost overnight Job sat alone among the ashes of his life, loathesomely and painfully ill, a pauper. Yet his faith was unshaken. "Shall we receive good at the hand of God," he admonished his wife, "and not receive evil?" (Job 2:10).

In recording this story in the Scriptures, the Holy Spirit has set forth for all time a clear and incisive statement concerning God's sovereignty over the lives of His children. The book of Job holds many other spiritual truths as well, but for the present, let us consider only God's supremacy over His people's suffering.

It was Satan, not God, who initiated Job's suffering, though God, for His own good reasons, allowed it and used it to bring Job into a deeper relationship with Himself. He also used it to instruct Christians of all time concerning His sovereignty and to foreshadow in the Old Testament His plan of redemption through suffering, which He later showed so clearly in the New. God also seems to have had some broader purpose in mind in allowing Job's affliction. For some reason which we can only dimly comprehend, the trial of Job's faith had cosmic significance to God and was precious in His sight.

But though Satan was permitted to afflict God's servant, it was God, not Satan, who laid down the rules of combat and drew up the battle lines. At no time did Satan challenge His right to this prerogative. At every point in this strange and bitter conflict, God, not Satan, was in control.

But God left Job in darkness concerning the strange drama that had sparked off the fiery spectacle in which he was called to be the principal actor. Nor did God tell Job what readers of the biblical story know from the outset, that Satan's power to afflict him was restricted by the hand of God. It must have seemed to Job that the unrestrained hostility of all hell was let loose upon him; yet all the while his torment was being monitored and controlled by the hand of the God he served and worshiped. Thus far would God suffer Satan to go, but no farther. Satan's power, great as it might be, was circumscribed by the sovereign power of God. Yet Job was denied the comfort of this knowledge in his hour of trial.

There was a day in the life of Job, good and godly man that he was, when his whole world caved in upon him. Such a day may come to any of us, and all too frequently it does. Paul's name for it was "the day of evil" (Eph. 6:13). We shall never have to suffer in the totality of darkness that Job knew, for we have the New Testament to light our way. Job suffered before the days of written Scripture. But God does not explain our trials to us any more than He did to Job, nor tell us what their significance is to Him; often our darkness is deep. From Job's story we learn that our faithfulness under unexplained pressure has meaning for God, and that God is no man's debtor. Job was faithful in his fiery ordeal and came to know God in a new way as a result. We may do the same.

Questions may be raised in our minds by some aspects of Job's story, particularly its final outcome, which sees Job restored to his former greatness, his flocks and herds doubled in number, the father of another family of seven sons and three daughters. Could a second family ever make up for the loss of a first one, we wonder?

God has not given us answers to such questions, and no one can call upon Him to justify His ways to man. "Shall not the Judge of all the earth do right?" If Christian faith means anything, it means that we must believe where we cannot see. Again and again in Scripture we see one person suffering in darkness for the benefit of others. Abraham, Noah, Joseph, Moses, Daniel, David, Paul — the list is a long one. Indeed, it is through such suffering that we know salvation today. The cross of Jesus illumines the darkness of our suffering. Christ is God's answer to the problem of human pain.

Our finite minds cannot fathom the infinite God. His ways are not our ways. His reasons are beyond our understanding. But, like Job, we trust the character of the God we worship. We believe with Wesley that "His nature and His name is Love." Our hearts trust the wisdom that our minds cannot comprehend.

And so we rest our questions as we read the story of Job, and take from it the sublime truth and comforting assurance that God wants all His children to grasp. Our God is sovereign. Though for His own inscrutable reasons He has allowed Satan temporary powers, He holds the reigns of government firmly in His own almighty hands.

Those hands were nailed to the cross for us. Why should we fear the suffering that Satan may bring into our lives? He can never overstep the boundaries laid down by our sovereign God, who has promised that He will not suffer us to be tempted beyond our ability to bear, and is even now working through our sorrows for His glory and our eternal good (1 Cor. 10:13; Rom. 8:28).

• 20 •

PERFECT THROUGH SUFFERINGS

IN THE FIRST CHAPTER OF THE BOOK OF HEBREWS, THE SPIRIT of God paints a vivid and majestic picture of the pre-incarnate Christ. He portrays Him in all the glories of His eternal and coequal existence with the Father, "God of God, Light of Light, very God of very God." He depicts Him in His mighty work of creation and redemption, finally ascribing to Him the seat of power at the right hand of the Father.

Then the picture changes. Before long we see Christ as the suffering servant of the Old Testament prophets. In startling language the Scriptures reveal the design by which God made Him to become the captain of our salvation: "In bringing many sons to glory, it was fitting that God, for whom and through whom everything exists, should make the author of their salvation perfect through suffering" (Heb. 2:10).

A little later we learn of Christ's ordination to the heavenly priesthood, where as our merciful and faithful high priest He appears in God's presence for us today: "Though he were a Son, yet learned he obedience by the things which he suffered; And being made perfect, he became the author of eternal salvation unto all them that obey him; Called of God an high priest after the order of Melchisedec" (Heb. 5:8-10 KJV).

Can these two pictures portray one and the same person? Can it really be that the coequal Son of the Father was made perfect through suffering, that the sharer of the eternal throne had to learn obedience by the things which He suffered?

This is what the Scriptures teach us, not only in these passages but in countless others. Through the prophets, God foretold the suffering servant of the Lord who should come to redeem His people. Alongside this picture He placed another, brighter one — that of the conquering King, great David's greater Son, who should come to free His captive people and establish His everlasting kingdom of justice and peace. Both were portraits of the Lord Jesus Christ.

But Israel did not understand that her Messiah must ascend His throne by the pathway of suffering, and so rejected Him. And although we Christians have the clear teaching of the New Testament to guide us, many of us have not really grasped this truth today. We may concede that suffering was a necessary part of the Redeemer's life, but we are less able — or willing — to see it as an integral part of our own. We would be stronger and more fruitful Christians if we did. We do not realize that because of man's fall, God has made suffering a part of His plan for His children, just as He did for His Son. Not that God wills suffering or wants it, but since man brought suffering on himself by his sin, God uses it to fulfill His redemptive purposes and to conform His people to the image of their Lord.

Was the Lord Jesus lacking in perfection that He had to learn obedience and be made perfect through suffering? Not at all. He was perfect as God is perfect, obedient from all eternity. As Son of God He needed no perfecting; but as Son of Man He had to be perfected for the work He had come to do, that He might become the perfect substitute, the perfect sacrifice, the perfect high priest for sinful man. In order to become man's Savior, His obedience had to be worked out in man's sinful world. As a man, the Savior had to learn the practice of obedience in the crucible of human suffering.

Suffering was no part of God's original creation; it was Satan's intrusion into man's life through man's fall. Jesus, though fully God, was also fully man. In order to redeem mankind, He had to live man's life to the utmost degree, and to bear in His body the full weight of man's sin. This meant that He had to experience the full weight of human suffering. In His life and sacrificial death, the Man of Sorrows learned perfect obedience in the fires of suffering, and so became our Savior and our great high priest.

The sovereign God took the suffering that man's sin had brought into the world and used it to perfect His sinless Son to accomplish man's redemption. He made Satan's intrusion the avenue by which the Savior attained His glory and ascended His throne. Should we, then, think it strange that He uses suffering to perfect His human children, to prepare them for the glorious destiny won for them by their suffering Lord?

• 21 •

SUFFERING AND GLORY

In the first chapter of Ephesians, the Holy Spirit reveals the glorious destiny God has prepared for His people. Ours is an astonishing prospect. We read that God chose us in Christ for a single purpose—to adopt us as His sons and make us like Jesus Christ. It is to this end that God had blessed us with all spiritual blessings in Christ, bestowing on us the redemption and forgiveness we so sorely need and sealing us with His Holy Spirit, who is our guarantor of the glorious inheritance we shall know in full in heaven. In Jesus Christ, God has destined His children for glory (Eph. 1:3-14).

The Lord Jesus is Himself the radiancy of God's glory and the express image of His person (Heb. 1:1-3). It is to His image that God, by His Holy Spirit, is conforming His children through all their earthly experiences: He is glorifying us, making us like Christ. How long, slow, and painful the process of transformation seems to be! But when Christ shall appear in glory, our internship will be ended. Then we shall be like Him, for we shall see Him as He is (1 John 3:2). This is the fullness of glory for which God has destined His people.

The eighth chapter of Romans teaches more about sonship and glory. "For you did not receive a spirit that makes you a slave again to fear," we read, "but you received the Spirit of sonship. And by him we cry 'Abba, Father.' The Spirit himself testifies with our spirit that we are God's children" (Rom. 8:15-16).

Then the Holy Spirit sounds a new note. The passage continues: "Now if we are children, then we are heirs—heirs of God and co-heirs with Christ, if indeed we share in his sufferings in order that we may also share in his glory. I consider that our present sufferings are not worth comparing with the glory that will be revealed in us" (Rom. 8:17-18).

Here the Holy Spirit is teaching us a profound truth: if God's children are to share in Christ's glory, they must also share in His sufferings. This is restated in Paul's letter to Timothy: "if we be dead with him, we shall also live with him; If we suffer, we shall also reign with him" (2 Tim. 2:11-12 KJV). The captain of our salvation came to His glory through suffering; we shall not know His glory any other way. Not that our suffering will in any way merit the glory we shall inherit; glory is the gift of God's free grace alone. What God is teaching here is that because of sin, glory is inextricably bound up with suffering. It is not possible to experience the one without the other. This was true for the Savior. The joy of bringing many sons to glory meant that He must first endure the cross (Heb. 2:19, 12:2). If God's holy Son had to be made perfect through suffering before attaining His glory, how can anything else be true for us?

God's purpose in choosing us, saving us, and destining us for glory is clarified in a thrice-repeated refrain found in the first chapter of Ephesians: we are to be *to the praise of God's glory,* to *show forth the praise of His glorious grace* (Eph. 1:6, 12, 14). If God's children are to demonstrate the praise of God's glory in heaven throughout eternity, it follows that our lives on earth must glorify Him too. And one of the areas in which we must learn to glorify God and reveal His nature is suffering. This, more than any other, was the way in which Christ glorified God. Not only in His gracious words and mighty acts, but supremely in His obedience, humiliation, suffering, and death did the Lord Jesus glorify His Father. Christ revealed God's nature and being to the world; in return, God set His seal of Sonship on the Lord Jesus and glorified Him as God.

We see this two-way glorification clearly as Christ approached His cross. Shortly before His crucifixion, He told His disciples that the hour had come for the Son of Man to be glorified. Then He went on to speak of the grain of wheat that must die in order to bring forth fruit and told His friends that this was the pathway both He and they must choose. Contemplating His imminent death, He exclaimed: " 'Now my heart is troubled, and what shall I say? "Father, save me from this hour"? No, it was for this very reason I came to this hour. *Father, glorify your name*!' Then a voice came from heaven, 'I have both glorified it, and will glorify it again'" (John 12:27-28). Jesus spoke of His suffering in terms of glory.

A little later, Judas went out to betray his Lord. To be betrayed by one of His own disciples must have been a particularly poignant sorrow to the Savior; but what did He say? "*'Now is the Son of Man glorified, and God is glorified in him'*" (John 13:31). Again He spoke not of suffering, but of glory. Then He went on to give the magnificent discourse contained in John 14-16.

We find the same theme of glory in the Garden of Gethsemane. Alone in His agony while His disciples slept, Jesus prayed, "'Father, the time has come. *Glorify your Son, that your Son may glorify you.* . . . I have brought you glory on earth by completing the work you gave me to do. And now, Father, glorify me in your presence with the glory I had with you before the world began'" (John 17:1, 4-5). And so Jesus went to the cross, glorifying God and being glorified Himself in His suffering.

Was God really glorified in Jesus' death? Our minds stagger at the thought. Was Jesus really glorifed, nailed naked and bleeding to a Roman cross? He announced His crucifixion by saying that the hour had come when He should be glorified. He began His last prayer on earth with the petition, "Father, glorify your Son, that your Son may glorify you." Clearly He knew that He would both glorify God and be glorified Himself in His death.

And never, indeed, was God so glorified as when the God-man Jesus Christ gave His life for the sins of the world. Never was God's love so clearly shown, His mercy and justice so surely demonstrated. Christ's glorification in His resurrection, ascension, and ultimate return in triumph would not have been possible had He not first glorified God and been glorified Himself on the cross. And there could have been no hope of glory for us.

The suffering that is part of our life is not a cruel, senseless waste. For the Christian, it has profound meaning. By it God is refining us and working for us an eternal weight of glory — the glory of being like Jesus Christ and living with Him forever. Through the very pain by which Satan seeks to destroy us, God is changing our sinful humanity into Christ's image, triumphing over Satan in us.

When we learn to rest our souls in these mighty truths, we know true peace. Our suffering takes on eternal dimensions. Our pain may not grow less, our loss may not be restored, our griefs may still be ours, but their power to harm us is broken. Our Savior glorified God by suffering in a human body and was glorified Himself as a result. God has a like purpose in our pain.

The Prince of Glory has not yet chosen to dazzle the world with the flashing forth of His glory; for the present He has chosen a humbler means of being glorified. When He prayed for those who should believe on Him He said, "Glory has come to me *through them*" (John 17:10). Suffering Christians are His means of showing God's glory to a watching world today. That means you and me.

Jesus came to His glory through suffering, and we must glorify Him in our suffering if we would share His glory in heaven. God will use the suffering that comes to us because of sin to declare His glory on earth, and to enable us to bear the glory of Christ's image in His presence throughout eternity. Shall we not say with Paul, "Our present sufferings are not worth comparing with the glory that will be revealed in us"?

• 22 •

GOD'S GLORY, AND OURS

WHAT IS GOD'S GLORY ANYWAY, YOU ASK? HOW CAN MY SUF-fering possibly glorify God? How on earth can suffering glorify me? These are valid questions. Let's turn to them now.

What is God's glory? It is the revelation of His essential being, of His character, of what He is. In Eden, God walked and talked with man as friend with friend, face to face. When man sinned, he lost the holy intimacy he was created to enjoy, for how could a holy God look on sin? Ever since man was cast out of Eden, no man can see God's face and live (Ex. 33:20).

But God has never ceased seeking to reveal and to communicate His being to man. He wants all men to know His glory, for in it His nature is disclosed. He knows that man's highest good consists in knowing his Creator and having fellowship with Him. God will never stop trying to make Himself known to His creation.

Over the centuries, God revealed His glory to His people in many ways. The glory of His presence led Israel through the desert with a pillar of cloud and fire. His glory crowned Mount Sinai as He gave the law. His Shekinah glory filled first the tabernacle in the wilderness, and later, Solomon's temple. To poets and prophets He gave special glimpses of His glory; and Isaiah sang of the day when the glory of the Lord should be revealed for all mankind to see (Isa. 40:5). This came to pass with the coming of Christ, when God's Word of love to man became flesh and lived among us, and we beheld His glory, full of grace and truth (John 1:14).

And through each successive revelation of God's glory, His people learned a little more of His character. They came to know His covenant care of His children, His abiding presence in their midst, His anger and judgment on their sin, His holiness, His righteousness, His majesty — and finally, in Christ, His redemptive love. Habakkuk and Isaiah envisioned as the culmination of all history that day when the earth should be filled with the knowledge of the glory of the Lord as the waters cover the sea (Hab. 2:14; Isa. 11:9).

Why does God desire that man should know His glory? It is not because He needs our worship, but because we need His grace; not to satisfy His ego, but to cover our sin and bring us back into that felicity of fellowship with Him for which we were created. God's glory is man's highest good. When we make it the supreme goal of our life, we will know the highest joys our natures can experience.

The disclosure of God's glory may be likened to the unfolding of a many-petalled rose, layer upon lovely layer. The bud shows only a promise of the wonders it encloses. But as the petals unfurl, the individual beauties of each part of the flower are revealed. We marvel at the intricacy of its design, the radiancy of its hues, the purity of its fragrance, until at last its golden heart lies open, not only for all to admire, but for pollination and the creation of new life. We find the very essence and nature of the rose in its full-blown blossom.

Jesus' revelation of God's glory was something like this. When He said that He had glorified God on the earth (John 17:4), He meant that He had revealed God's nature to mankind. As with the rose, man saw the very essence and nature of God in Jesus Christ. Those who witnessed His life and heard His words saw what God was like. Jesus glorified, or revealed, God; and God was glorified, or displayed, in Christ. And in return, God glorified Jesus. He acknowledged His Sonship and supremacy before earth and heaven and hell in His resurrection, ascension, and exaltation; one day He will consummate His glory in His triumphal return as King.

In a similar way, Christians are meant to glorify God and to be themselves glorified by Him. We are to reveal God's nature to a world that doesn't know Him. We are to show God's power at work in human lives and circumstances and to manifest His victory. We are to display Christ's character being slowly but surely formed in us by His Holy Spirit. This is what it means to be to the praise of God's glory, which is our destiny in Christ Jesus. As the petals unfolding reveal the rose, so, one by one, day by day, hour by hour, we Christians are to disclose the attributes of God to men.

To seek to fulfill such a destiny is no small task. It is the work of a lifetime and will not be fully accomplished until we see our Savior face to face. Yet if we will allow Him, God's Spirit at work within us will gradually reveal His glory through our lives. Men and angels and demons will become aware of God's character as they see His nature displayed in us. And all the while, as we glorify God day by day, His spirit will be working to glorify us — forming Christ's likeness in us, restoring in us the clarity of the image of God which is distorted by our sin. When Christ returns and we see Him as He is, we shall be like Him, perfect in holiness, made ready to share His eternal glory.

How can our suffering glorify God? Though the whole of our lives is meant to be lived to God's glory, suffering is a touchstone in human experience. If we can glorify God there, we are likely to be able to glorify Him anywhere. So the New Testament has quite a lot to say about glorifying God in suffering. Its outworking is a practical thing. Whenever a Christian is found faithful in the crucible of suffering, patient and steadfast in affliction and trial, gentle and long-suffering when falsely accused or reviled, able to repay evil with good and hatred with love, there God is glorified. His nature is revealed before the world, for it is not in human nature to react to suffering in this manner. God's power and holiness are displayed in us; Christ's victory is vindicated; Satan is rebuked and cast down. And at the same time, the sufferers themselves are being glorified as God forms His own life ever more surely and clearly in their souls.

Suffering will come to all of us in this life; none can hope to escape it. Christian and non-Christian alike must share in the pain of the universe. But only we who are Christians can know meaning in our pain. We alone, of all sufferers, can suffer in hope of the glory of God. God does not will us to suffer, but He uses the suffering that is ours to reveal Himself to an unbelieving world and to prepare His children for the glory He is preparing for them in heaven. Meanwhile, the world about us suffers in despair and darkness.

God does not use His people's suffering to magnify His glory because of any need of His, but because of our need. All honor and praise are His; man cannot add to His glory. But He knows, far better than we do, the extremities of our need in the face of human suffering. In mercy and in grace, He offers us His succor and hope in place of darkness and desolation.

We may work with God to allow Him to bring His glory out of our suffering, or we may resist Him and frustrate His purposes for us. In either case, we will suffer, for suffering is the common lot of humanity. But how sad to suffer without hope when God means us to rejoice in the hope that His glory and our eternal good are being worked out through our pain!

May we seek God's grace that we may lose nothing of the glory God has for us in our suffering!

• 23 •

IS SUFFERING GOD'S GIFT?

IS SUFFERING REALLY GOD'S GIFT? THERE ARE THOSE WHO claim that it is. Some even insist that the sufferer — always someone else! — must thank God for his pain. Countless suffering Christians, already borne down by sorrow, know additional torment because of well-meaning friends who press them to accept such views.

We all know Christians whose lives are overshadowed, perhaps almost eclipsed, by some problem of pain. We may even carry such a burden ourselves. Most of us have read or heard of the young quadriplegic Joni Eareckson who was paralyzed from the neck down in a diving accident in 1967 at the age of seventeen. She has spent her life since that time in a wheelchair, totally helpless, unable even to blow her own nose; yet her radiant spirit is an inspiration and rebuke to all who know her.

How can we explain such devastation? Does God really send such suffering to those He loves? Is Joni's pain really His gift? How can we reconcile such a view with His biblical revelation of Himself as a loving, omnipotent Father whose gifts are good and perfect?

The Oxford Dictionary defines *gift* as "the voluntary transference of property without consideration; a present." A present is something we give as a mark of affection in order to bring pleasure to another. It must be our property before we can give it. Suffering is not a property of God, but of Satan. Its intent is not pleasure, but pain. Suffering can never be truly a gift of God.

Those who maintain that God is the giver of afflictions such as Joni's — or yours — lay a cruel, almost intolerable burden on sensitive spirits. Because such teaching is a half-truth, its error is more dangerous than an outright lie. It enables the Deceiver to present a distorted image of God: Is *this* the way a loving Father treats His children? It gives the Accuser opportunity to torture cleansed consciences by creating false guilt: You must be terribly wicked to deserve such a gift as this!

Proponents of this perverted view base their arguments on a few proof texts, considering them in isolation rather than within the content of the whole body of revealed truth. Such persons malign the nature of God, for in using the word *giver* as if it were synonymous with *originator,* they effectively portray God as the author of evil.

It is true that our pain comes to us only as God allows it. In this sense, and this sense only, He may be said to "give" it. But suffering originates with Satan. It entered man's life only after his sin. It is part of sin's curse, under which we must live until Christ comes to set up His righteous kingdom. God allows suffering and uses it, but it is not His gift; His gift is the work He accomplishes through it, the grace He gives to triumph over it, and His presence with the sufferer in his sorrow.

One verse by which some seek to prove that suffering is God's gift is Philippians 1:29: "For it has been granted to you on behalf of Christ, not only to believe on him, but also to suffer for him." What is the context in which this statement appears? Paul has been speaking of his imprisonment, saying that it had actually served to advance the cause of the Gospel. Everyone knew that he was in chains for Christ's sake, he says, and this had encouraged many Christians to speak the Gospel more fearlessly. He goes on to encourage the Philippian Christians to refuse to be terrified by their own adversaries, for all Christians must expect to face Satan's opposition in one way or another. Persecution and suffering are part and parcel of being a Christian.

Paul is merely saying here what he also says in Romans 8:17 — that as we hope to share Christ's glory, we will also share His sufferings; and again in 2 Timothy 2:12 — that if we endure with Christ we shall also reign with Him. This is the consistent teaching of the Scriptures. It is what Peter means when he writes that we are "called" to suffer (1 Pet. 2:21).

The whole thrust of the apostle's teaching in verses like these is that suffering will be an integral part of life for the Christian as it was for his Lord, that God will use this suffering, and that it will be followed by glory — a clearer revelation of God. If some wish to consider their sufferings as gifts from God, at least they should not force their views on other sufferers. It is not only unbiblical, but cruel to do so.

Suffering formed a large part of the life of the Apostle Paul. Why was it "given" to him? Was it the gift of God's love?

After Paul's encounter with the risen Christ on the Damascus Road, God sent Ananias to minister to him. He told Ananias that Paul had been chosen for a special task — that of carrying His name before the Gentiles and their kings, as well as before Israel. He concluded with a strange statement: "I will show him [Paul] how much he must suffer for my name" (Acts 9:16).

Obviously part of the equipment for Paul's special task was to be suffering. God's work had to be done, and for reasons we only dimly discern, suffering was to be one of the ways by which His purpose for and through Paul would be realized. To that extent, we may say that God "gave" suffering to Paul, even as He did to Christ.

But Paul's suffering was not God's gift in the sense that God wanted Paul to suffer, any more than He wanted Jesus to suffer. Because of man's sin, such suffering was a necessity if God's saving purpose was to be accomplished. God's gift was not suffering, but salvation; suffering was merely a means to that end. We may imagine that God "gave" it to Paul, as, indeed He does to us, only with the greatest reluctance. But the fact that the Gentiles are Christians today is testimony to the effectiveness of God's work accomplished through Paul's suffering.

Later, Paul writes about his ecstatic experience. He was caught up to paradise and heard inexpressible things he could not even talk about. But he continues, "To keep me from becoming conceited because of these surpassingly great revelations, there was given me a thorn in my flesh, a messenger of Satan, to torment me. Three times I pleaded with the Lord to take it away from me. But He said to me, 'My grace is sufficient for you, for my power is made perfect in weakness'" (2 Cor. 12:7-9).

We notice that although God allowed this thorn to be given to Paul, yet the Holy Spirit, in recording the story, calls it "a messenger of Satan" the purpose of which — the torment of Paul — was evil, not good. God may have "given" it (although the Scriptures do not actually say so), but He makes it very clear that it had originated with Satan. Once again, God is using Satan's evil to work out His own purposes.

And though Paul besought the Lord three times to remove the thorn, God did not see fit to do so. Instead, He gave His servant two rich gifts — His grace, in measure sufficient to enable Paul to triumph over his suffering, and the outworking of His own strength coming to maturity in Paul through the weakness caused by his affliction. Paul came to value God's gifts so highly that eventually he delighted in the infirmity that had brought them into his life.

And so it may be with us as we suffer today. Those who see God at work in their trials and seek to realize the richness of His grace and presence through them often come to find in their trouble something for which to be profoundly thankful. But such gratitude is for God's gifts of grace, for the revelation of Himself that He gives in suffering, not for the sorrow itself. God does not require us to thank Him for that nor to cherish it as a gift. He knows better than we do that it is evil.

Pain is pain and sorrow is sorrow. It hurts. It limits. It impoverishes. It isolates. It restrains. It works devastation deep within the personality. It circumscribes us in a thousand bitter ways. There is nothing good about it. But the gifts God can give with it are the richest the human spirit can know. Joni's paralysis and wheelchair are the enemy's work, but God's gift is His grace, His "way of escape" which does not remove her helplessness but makes her triumphant over it.

Only eternity can tell why God allowed a lovely young teenager like Joni to suffer such stark tragedy — or why you suffer today. But His victory over sin is evident in Joni's radiant spirit, and can be experienced in yours. God has made of Joni a rare and precious jewel, chiseled and burnished by pain. Through her the riches of His grace are being displayed before thousands on earth and untold thousands of witnesses in the heavenly places. Before her testimony Satan is daily being shown up for the liar that he is, while God is being glorified as His power and grace are being revealed. Joni, like Job, has a place in God's eternal plan.

And so have you — and I. Let us not thwart Him, but rest in our sovereign God to work His good through the evil that Satan sends into our lives!

• 24 •

SUFFERING AND JUDGMENT

"IS MY SUFFERING GOD'S JUDGMENT ON ME BECAUSE OF SIN? IS He punishing me for something I may have done, perhaps long ago?" How many an anguished sufferer is tormented by such questions when catastrophe strikes! How human it is to feel guilty in the face of unexplained suffering! And how the Accuser delights to saddle God's children with burdens of false guilt!

What is the relationship between suffering and judgment? This is a question which must be considered in any biblical study of the problem of pain.

It is true that the Scriptures cite instances of both individual and national suffering because of God's judgment on sin, but it is equally true that they do not teach that all suffering is of this kind. The biblical record demonstrates that the pain of the universe, in which all mankind must share, is experienced in many different ways which may arise from a variety of causes. Scriptural examples of physical suffering range from the extreme of demon possession to ordinary infirmities, from congenital blindness, which Jesus said was in order that God's work might be made visible (John 9), to premature death, which He said was that God's glory might be revealed (John 11). Job was declared to be righteous by God Himself, yet Job suffered acutely as did many other upright servants of God.

We must beware of thinking that because some suffering may be the result of personal sin, therefore all suffering is of that kind. It is a logical fallacy to assume that because all cats are animals, therefore all animals are cats. We must refuse to entertain such fallacies regarding suffering. Their origin is Satanic; they are traps set to destroy us.

Some passages of Scripture do indeed seem to show God's judgment falling on particular people because of particular sins — sins of which such individuals were fully aware. Examples of God's

74

particular judgment may be the fate of Lot's wife; the death of Achan and his family; Gehazi's leprosy; Saul's rejection as king; the death of Bathsheba's baby and the sword drawn in the household of David; Zacharias's dumbness; the deaths of Ananias and Sapphira.

It is important, however, to distinguish between suffering as judgment for sin and suffering as the consequence of sin. Implicit in God's judgment against sin in general is the simple law of cause and effect: sin gives rise to consequences for those who indulge in it. Just as it is with the laws of our country, if we transgress against God's natural, moral, or spiritual laws, we will suffer the inevitable consequences. God's judgment is set against sin itself rather than against the sinner. If we sin willfully and persistently, we invite the consequences that must follow sin, and this will involve suffering. Perhaps it is more accurate to say that the persons noted above did not suffer God's punishment for their sin so much as sin's inescapable consequences. God's righteous judgment fell on their sin, and they suffered as a result.

Satan, however, delights to make us feel that our suffering is God's punishment for sin. He is the Deceiver, the Arch-Accuser who is forever seeking to rob us of God's gift of a cleansed conscience, and so to render us powerless in our Christian walk and witness.

What is the teaching of Scripture concerning God's children and sin? John summarizes it clearly in his first letter. "If we say that we have no sin, we deceive ourselves, and the truth is not in us. ... And if any man sin, we have an advocate with the Father, Jesus Christ the righteous. ... If we confess our sins, he is faithful and just to forgive us our sins, and to cleanse us from all unrighteousness. ... If we walk in the light, as he is in the light, we have fellowship one with another, and the blood of Jesus Christ his Son cleanseth us [keeps on cleansing us] from all sin" (1 John 1:8, 2:1, 1:9, 1:7 KJV).

God laid the punishment for our sins on the Lord Jesus. That satisfied both His holiness and His justice; He cannot now rightly punish us as well. When we come to Him in faith, confessing our sins, God forgives them and forgets them; they are no more. If, however, we persist in sin of which we are fully aware, refusing to forsake it, God may let His judgment fall on our sin and we may suffer as a result. But this is something that is in our power to prevent; it cannot come about unless we set the stage for it. It is a form of suffering that we bring upon ourselves.

Satan, however, Deceiver and Accuser that he is, seeks to confuse us on this issue, as we saw in Chapter 16. He tries to convince us that all our sufferings are God's punishment for our sin, haunting us with vague, distressing feelings of fear and guilt as he seeks to cripple us spiritually. We must learn to rebuke and resist the Accuser and to recognize and respond to the promptings of the Holy Spirit who seeks to lead us to repentance, restoration, and a renewal of fellowship.

Sometimes a well-meaning but misguided Christian will make bold to approach a suffering fellow-Christian in the manner of Job's comforters — telling him that he must be suffering because of some secret sin he is harboring and urging him to confess and forsake it and so be healed. Only God knows the spiritual damage that can result from such rash action. We must beware of ever pointing a finger at another's suffering and calling it judgment for sin. This is God's responsibility, not ours. The only sin we have to concern ourselves with is our own.

Jesus clearly warned against such presumptuous behavior in His teaching about the Galileans whose blood Herod had mingled with their sacrifices, and again about the eighteen persons who were killed by a falling tower in Siloam (Luke 13:1-5). His word to those who dared to suggest that their fate was a judgment for personal sin was a categorical "I tell you, No! But unless you repent, you too will all perish!" A similar teaching comes also in John 9; in answer to a question concerning the cause of blindness in the man born blind, Jesus replied that the cause was neither the sin of the man himself nor that of his parents, but that God's glory should be made known. Then the Savior simultaneously revealed God's glory and proved Himself to be the Light of the world by giving first physical and then spiritual light to the man born to darkness. We must be very slow to attribute suffering to any sin other than our own.

But each of us must look to ourselves in this regard. Paul teaches this very clearly. "Do not be deceived: God cannot be mocked," he tells us. "A man reaps what he sows. The one who sows to please his sinful nature, from that nature will reap destruction; the one who sows to please the Spirit, from the Spirit will reap eternal life. Let us not become weary in doing good, for at the proper time we will reap a harvest if we do not give up" (Gal. 6:7-9). We must constantly be on the watch in our own lives lest we should sow the wind and, as a result, reap the whirlwind (Hos. 8:7).

When suffering comes to us we must not rule out the possibility of judgment for sin. We must ask the Holy Spirit to try our hearts and to search out any sin we may have hidden, even from ourselves, that could be a cause of our affliction. If He convicts us of something, however trivial, we must deal with it at once. If, on the other hand, the Accuser seeks to torment us with false guilt about vague generalities, or about sins we have confessed and for which we have been forgiven, we must resist him with the Word of God until he flees from us. We need listen only to the Spirit, never the Accuser.

Our God is a God of mercy as well of a judgment; and as Milton says, His "Mercy first and last shall brightest shine" (*Paradise Lost,* Bk. III, l. 134). "The Lord is merciful and gracious, slow to anger, and plenteous in mercy. He will not always chide: neither will he keep his anger for ever. He hath not dealt with us after our sins; nor rewarded us according to our iniquities. For as the heaven is high above the earth, so great is his mercy toward them that fear him. As far as the east is from the west, so far hath he removed our transgressions from us. Like as a father pitieth his children, so the Lord pitieth them that fear him. For he knoweth our frame; he remembereth that we are dust" (Psa. 103:8-14 KJV).

The witness of all Scripture is that God's judgments are saving judgments. If His hand is heavy upon us because of some sin, it is only that we may recognize it, repent of it, confess it, and know the mercy of His forgiveness and restoring grace.

• 25 •

SUFFERING AS CHASTISEMENT

ANOTHER REASON GOD MAY SEND SUFFERING INTO THE LIVES of His children is for disciplinary training or chastisement. The Scriptures have quite a bit to say about this kind of suffering. Their teaching is clear and unmistakable.

Moses referred to such chastisement in his farewell charge to Israel. Among the things he asked the people to remember after his death was God's fatherly chastening of His covenant people. "Know then in your heart that as a man disciplines his son, so the Lord your God disciplines you," he admonished (Deut. 8:5). Solomon counseled his sons to heed God's chastisement and to profit from it: "My son, do not despise the Lord's discipline and do not resent his rebuke, because the Lord disciplines those he loves, as a father the son he delights in" (Prov. 3:11-12). And David acknowledged the value of God's discipline and exclaimed: "Thou hast dealt well with thy servant, O Lord, according to thy word. . . . Before I was afflicted I went astray; but now I keep thy word. . . . I know, O Lord, that thy judgments are right, and that in faithfulness thou hast afflicted me" (Psa. 119:65, 67, 75 RSV).

The writer to the Hebrew Christians speaks of God's disciplinary chastisement as he urges perseverance on the members of the young church: "In your struggle against sin, you have not yet resisted to the point of shedding your blood. And you have forgotten that word of encouragement that addresses you as sons: 'My son, do not make light of the Lord's discipline, and do not lose heart when he rebukes you, because the Lord disciplines those he loves, and he punishes everyone he accepts as a son.' Endure hardship as discipline; God is treating you as sons. For what son is not disciplined by his father? If you are not disciplined (and everyone undergoes discipline), then you are illegitimate children and not true sons. Moreover, we have all had human fathers who disciplined us and we respected them for it. How much more should we submit to the Father of our spirits and live! Our fathers disciplined us for a little while as they thought best; but God disciplines us for our good, that we may share in his holiness. No discipline seems pleasant at the time, but painful. Later on, however, it produces a harvest of righteousness and peace for those who have been trained by it" (Heb. 12:4-11).

Paul sees suffering as a cause for rejoicing because of the benefits God will work for us through it: "We rejoice in our sufferings, because we know that suffering produces perseverance; perseverance, character; and character, hope. And hope does not disappoint us, because God has poured his love into our hearts by the Holy Spirit, whom he has given us" (Rom. 5:3-5). He goes on to expand on the magnitude of that love whose riches we have come to know more fully through our suffering: "Who shall separate us from the love of Christ? Shall trouble or hardship or persecution or famine or nakedness or danger or sword? ... No, in all these things we are more than conquerors through him who loved us. For I am convinced that neither death nor life, neither angels nor demons, neither the present nor the future, nor any powers, neither height nor depth, nor anything else in all creation, will be able to separate us from the love of God that is in Christ Jesus our Lord" (Rom. 8:35, 37-39). These are some of the blessings of God's disciplinary training.

God's chastisement is not judgment on sin, but rather disciplinary correction. It is not administered in anger, but in purest love. A wise parent will "punish" a child in order to train him, to help him to remember what will result from breaking some natural law, or to impress on him the gravity of an offence so he will not repeat it. This helps to turn his young footsteps in the desired pathway of health and happiness. If such chastisement is wisely and lovingly administered, even a very young child will understand it and turn to his father's way. Every good parent and teacher has proved the truth of this.

And that is what God's chastisement is — not punishment, but training in His ways. Our wise, loving Father, who sees the end from the beginning, seeks to turn us from our waywardness into His paths of righteousness and peace. He knows the awful end of our ways and the eternal blessedness of His.

How we humans do love to go our own way! Even the regenerate human heart does not turn easily from its own way to

God's way. But the end of our way is death. God is constantly turning our footsteps back into His own life-giving way. Is not this where we most truly desire to go? Then why should we shrink from His training? When suffering comes, shall we not rather look up to Him in faith and ask Him to teach us all that He wishes us to learn through our trial?

How much God's children have learned in His school of suffering! Spiritual truths we could not have come to understand in any other way have been made plain to us in times of pain and trouble. God has set forth His truth in His Word for our learning, but often we are unwilling or unable to accept it until suffering throws us back on God in such need that we become willing to allow the Holy Spirit to teach us and to validate in our experience the things that God has been longing that we should learn.

Let us look at our suffering as part of our Father's wise and loving child-training, which fulfills His purpose of conforming us to the image of His Son and prepares us for the glory of holy sonship for which He has chosen us in Christ Jesus!

· 26 ·

SUFFERING AS A TRIAL OF FAITH

FROM EARLIEST TIMES, GOD HAS TESTED HIS CHILDREN WITH suffering of one kind or another in order to try their faith and equip them to carry greater responsibilities in His work of bringing His eternal purposes to pass.

He asked Noah to withstand the jeers of his godless neighbors while for 120 long, hard years, on dry land far from the sea, he worked at building an enormous and seemingly ridiculous and useless ark.

He promised Abraham that He would make him the father of many nations, but kept him childless until he was one hundred years old. Then when He gave him the child of His promise, He asked him to offer his beloved son Isaac up as a sacrifice.

He gave Joseph dreams of future greatness and then allowed him to be sold by his jealous brothers as a slave into Egypt. When His faithful servant honored God by withstanding the temptations of Potiphar's wife, He left him to languish for long years forgotten in prison.

He led Moses to leave his privileged position as a member of Pharaoh's household and identify himself with his enslaved Hebrew people only to be rejected as their leader and have to spend forty years tending sheep in the wilderness of Midian.

He anointed the boy David as king of Israel and gave him the spirit of a king, only to leave him wandering for years with a price on his head, a hunted, homeless refugee.

These men were among God's choicest saints; yet in these and countless other cases, God tested and trained His servants through long years of affliction before finally moving to accomplish His purposes through them.

But accomplish them He did. Noah saved the race from extinction in the flood, thereby enabling God to fulfill the promise of redemption He had given in Eden. Abraham became the father

81

of the Jewish nation, through which God gave to the world the Scriptures and the Redeemer, His written and His living Word. Joseph saved the infant nation Israel from starving to death when famine ravaged that part of the world. Moses led God's people out of bondage in Egypt to a life of freedom in the wilderness until they entered the land God had promised to Abraham; he also gave them God's law and the Levitical form of worship, which prefigured the work of Christ. David became the greatest of all the kings of Israel and was the prototype of the greater Son of David whose throne shall stand forever and whose kingdom shall know no end. When God finally put these people in the place of responsibility where eternal issues hung in the balance, He had developed their faith until it was strong enough to stand the test.

God still tests His children in order to fit us for our place in His plan and to work His will through us. Suffering is still one of His tools. Often He asks us to suffer in the dark, as He did with His saints of old, promising us good but allowing us only apparent evil. Only by such pressure can He strengthen and fit sinful humans for His use. Is it not the pressure of untold centuries that transforms common carbon until it flashes with the iridescence of flawless diamonds? Only by similar testing can God refine our feeble faith until it is strong enough to embrace His purposes and do His will.

The Apostles Peter and James taught that such testing is a cause for joy. "Dear friends, do not be surprised at the painful trial you are suffering, as though something strange were happening to you," Peter wrote to the early church. "But rejoice that you participate in the sufferings of Christ, so that you may be overjoyed when his glory is revealed" (1 Pet. 4:12). He warns them to expect such suffering: "now for a little while you may have to suffer various trials, so that the genuineness of your faith, more precious than gold which though perishable is tested by fire, may redound to praise and glory and honor at the revelation of Jesus Christ" (1 Pet. 1:6-7 RSV).

James begins his letter with similar teaching: "Consider it pure joy, my brothers, whenever you face trials of many kinds, because you know that the testing of your faith develops perseverance. Perseverance must finish its work so that you may be mature and complete, not lacking anything. . . . Blessed is the man who perseveres under trial, because when he has stood the test, he will receive the crown of life that God has promised to those who love him" (James 1:2-4, 12).

The apostles were thinking primarily of the persecutions that were already threatening the early Christians under Nero and others when they wrote these words, but their truths apply to Christians of any era. God is accomplishing His eternal purposes through Christians whose faith He has tested and tempered like steel. Suffering is one of the means by which He perfects His work of faith in His people. And the trial of our faith is precious in God's sight.

An early psalmist learned this long ago: "For you, O God, tested us; you refined us like silver. You brought us into prison and laid burdens on our backs. You let men ride over our heads; we went through fire and water, but you brought us to a place of abundance" (Psa. 66:10-12).

As we have seen, God is not the author of suffering. He did not intend that mankind should suffer. But because of man's sin, suffering is now a part of our human heritage. Rather than let it ravage His people in wild and useless waste, God in His economy harnesses suffering and turns it to the perfecting of His own designs. The wise Christian is he who aligns himself with his Creator in His purposes, and so does not suffer in vain.

It is possible that your suffering today may be God's trying of your faith in order to equip you for greater responsibilities in His service. Trust Him, and serve Him faithfully and uncomplainingly. One day, His purpose accomplished, you will shine with the glory of Christ's likeness before your Father's face.

• 27 •

SUFFERING AS THE REFINER'S FIRE

ANOTHER WAY GOD USES SUFFERING IS TO REFINE AND PURIFY His people. The messenger who came to prepare the way of the Lord (Mal. 3:1-4) was sent "to purify the Levites" until they should present "offerings in righteousness . . . acceptable to the Lord." God still refines His people to fit them for purer service. Sometimes He uses suffering as His messenger.

How often we serve God in our own strength, bringing Him our own puny offerings! He wants to prepare us for truer service and higher offerings. He allows suffering to come into our lives. "I will bring [them] into the fire; I will refine them like silver," He says, "and test them like gold" (Zech. 13:9). So He purifies the relationship between Himself and His people until He is able to say, "They will call on my name, and I will answer them; I will say, 'They are my people,' and they will say, 'The Lord is our God.'"

Gold and silver are precious metals. We refine them to make them more suited to the needs for which we wish to use them. Only refined gold is useful gold. God refines His people for the same reason. But how does suffering refine God's children?

Suffering purifies. When we are in pain, we are willing to let go of all that cannot stand the fiery test. We come to see ourselves for what we are — helpless, hurting, weakened by sin. We cry to God for wholeness, and this is the first step towards holiness.

Suffering clarifies our sense of values. It forces us to choose between reality and illusion, between what we are and what we think we are, between what we need and what we think we need; it crystallizes our faith. We learn what we really believe and why; we let go of our own pet notions and throw ourselves upon God's truth.

Suffering may be a means of growth. It hurls us utterly on God and teaches us to trust Him. In the crucible of suffering we learn our true identity. We are enabled to look up into God's face and to say with certainty and finality, *"The Lord is my God"* — and to mean it. The Lord Jesus was Himself refined — made perfect — through sufferings. Shall we wonder, then, if suffering is a part of our lives? How else could we become like our suffering Lord?

With us in the refiner's fire, as with Shadrach, Meshach, and Abednego in the Chaldean furnace, walks the Son of God. In fellowship with Him, we shall find that the fire has no power against us; not even the smell of smoke will linger about us (Dan. 3:27).

God Himself entered our suffering in the person of His suffering Son, thereby sanctifying forever all human pain. Before the throne today Jesus wears our human body, the marks of suffering still visible upon it. There He intercedes for us continually, sending His grace to enable us to triumph in our pain. It is no stranger who holds the crucible of our suffering, but our own beloved Lord. "See, I have refined you, though not as silver," He whispers to us; "I have tested you in the furnace of affliction" (Isa. 48:10). One day we shall appear before Him pure and holy, perfectly fitted to serve Him throughout eternity.

• 28 •

SUFFERING FOR GOD'S GLORY

THERE ARE MANY REASONS WHY GOD'S CHILDREN MAY undergo severe trials. One of the least understood of these is cosmic in nature. Job's sufferings were of this kind.

Through Job's faithfulness in his undeserved and unexplained afflictions, God was enabled to humble proud Satan before all the hosts of hell and heaven and to display His own power and glory. Hostile and rebellious principalities and powers were made to bow before this demonstration of God's might and wisdom. Job himself was given a transcendent vision of God that transformed his whole life. God's people have had clearer insights into the mystery of suffering ever since, and surer knowledge of immortality. And Old Testament worshipers were given a glimpse of the redemption through suffering that Jesus would disclose fully only centuries later.

We have already noted Jesus' statement that the man born blind was imprisoned in darkness for long years in order that God's glory might be displayed in his healing (John 9:3). Lazarus's death and resurrection would seem to be of the same order (John 11).

Lazarus's suffering and death, and the sufferings of his family—sufferings all made more acute by the seeming indifference of their Lord—were for the glory of God (vv. 4, 40, 45). In raising Lazarus from his four-day grave, Jesus gave indisputable proof of God's power over death, thereby giving substance and meaning to the mighty words that have whispered hope to countless sufferers ever since—His great statement concerning the certainty of life after death: "I am the resurrection and the life. He who believes in me will live, even though he dies; and whoever lives and believes in me will never die" (John 11: 25-26).

Some of God's saints may be suffering for reasons of this kind today, although they will not be aware of it. Joni's paralysis and overcoming grace may indeed be closely akin to Job's afflictions and perseverance. Without a doubt, God is enabling Joni to triumph in her devastation, and so to witness to the glory of His power and grace not only before thousands here on earth, but before untold thousands of cosmic intelligences in the invisible sphere of spiritual reality. It may be that this is the real reason, perhaps the only reason, for Joni's sufferings.

No one can know that his suffering is of cosmic significance. While any sorrow nobly borne brings honor to God inasmuch as it displays His sustaining power and so reveals His nature, only God Himself knows whose pain is designed for cosmic reasons. But even today He has His Job-like witnesses on earth, one here, one there, faithful in the midst of affliction, proving His sufficiency before a mighty cloud of observers. Only He knows the significance of such evidence, but by faith we embrace His purpose and trust Him to help us do our part in fulfilling it if that is what He asks us to do, difficult as that may be.

Perhaps the greatest good that suffering can work for a believer is to increase the capacity of his soul for God. Only when we are at the end of our own resources will many of us draw upon the wealth God longs to give us. As pain forces us to the limits of our own endurance, we come to discover God's strength; as it empties us of ourselves, we begin to experience God's fullness. The greater our need, the greater will be our capacity; the greater our capacity, the greater will be our experience of God.

And not only is this true on earth, it is supremely true in heaven. In that day when we shall be filled with all the fullness of God, surely those who have the greatest capacity for God will know His fullness in greatest measure. Can any price be too much to pay for such eternal good?

It is possible that your suffering today, or mine, may be sent for one of God's inscrutable but cosmic reasons. What higher calling can anyone know than to be to the praise of God's glory, even if it must be by suffering? If this is what God asks of us, may we be found faithful.

• 29 •

FILLING UP CHRIST'S SUFFERINGS

ON THE FIRST PAGE OF PAUL'S LETTER TO THE COLOSSIANS we find a surprising statement: "I rejoice in sufferings for your sake," the Apostle writes to the young church, "and in my flesh I complete what is lacking in Christ's afflictions for the sake of his body, that is, the church" (Col. 1:24 RSV). What can these words mean? Are Christ's sufferings, through which alone we receive salvation, not complete? Is there something lacking in them that we as Christians are meant to perfect?

The answer to this question is both Yes and No. Certainly Christ's sufferings are complete as far as our redemption is concerned. When He cried "It is finished!" His work was ended. His death completely atones for sin. Nothing we can ever do can add to His suffering or affect its efficacy. We are totally dependent on Christ's work for our salvation. But in several places the Scriptures teach that our sufferings, like His, may have significance for the church, His body. As with so many things concerning our salvation, this is a mystery. But it is a mystery in which all Christians have some part, and in which some of us may have a special part.

The Word of God has a number of things to say about suffering that "fills up" Christ's afflictions. In 2 Corinthians 1:3-7 we read of one way in which the sufferings of Christians are meant to benefit others as well as themselves. Paul says that God will comfort us in our sufferings, for all who share Christ's sufferings will also share His comforts. But he makes it clear that God does not impart His consolations to help only those who are suffering, but for the sake of His whole church; they are meant to be shared. "If we are distressed," writes Paul, "it is for your comfort and salvation; and if we are comforted, it is for your comfort" (v. 6). Christians are all bound up together in Christ's body; they share His suffering and His comforts. How often have we been encouraged and strengthened in sorrow by God's comforts mediated to us through the words of other Christians! This is one of God's ways of using the suffering of one of His children to benefit another.

It should be no surprise to Christ's followers to learn that they must share His sufferings. Jesus made this clear to His disciples, telling them that they would indeed "drink the cup" and share His baptism of pain (Mark 10:39); that they would know His sorrow, but that it would be turned into joy (John 16:20). In His discourse concerning the end of the age, He taught that the birth-pangs that would precede His return would be shared by His church (Matt. 24:21-22). This was foretold by Daniel (Dan. 12:1) and foreseen by John in his apocalyptic vision (Rev. 12:1-3, 13-17). Paul taught that it was through many hardships that we should enter the kingdom of God (Acts 14:22). There are more promises concerning suffering in the New Testament than there are promises of prosperity and earthly well-being. God did not save us primarily to make us happy or healthy or prosperous, but to make us holy. Why should God's people expect to escape suffering? God has told us very clearly that He will use the suffering that Satan has wrought through man's sin to accomplish His purposes.

We have noted earlier that if we are God's children, then we are heirs of Christ's glory, and that if we are to share in that glory, we must also share in Christ's suffering (Rom. 8:17). God has told us that His purpose in adopting us as His sons is to shape us to Christ's image (Rom. 8:29; Eph. 1:4-5). How could we be made like the Lord Jesus if we did not share His suffering as well as His risen life?

Paul prayed that he might know Christ and the power of His resurrection (Phil. 3:10). Many of us would pray a like prayer; fewer of us, however, would go on to pray, as Paul does, that we may know Christ's resurrection power by sharing in His death. We'd all like to experience resurrection power without first suffering spiritual death, but this is not God's way.

Only the sovereignty of God could make of the sufferings that are ours because of sin a means of knowing Christ and sharing in His risen life. Only the wisdom of God could take the sufferings that His sinful creatures cannot hope to avoid and make them a means of nourishing His church. Only the humility and grace of God could honor His feeble saints by using their sufferings to "complete," or "fill up," the sufferings of His holy Son.

How are Christ's sufferings "completed" by ours? In His death and resurrection, Christ demonstrated God's triumph over the powers of evil. His sufferings will only be "completed" when His people display that same victory in their own lives. This can only take place as they learn to share Christ's sufferings and death. By manifesting before the cosmic forces the reality of Christ's conquest over sin amidst the pressures of human life in a sinful world, we are "completing" Christ's sufferings, showing their validity for the here and now.

Such vindication of God's purposes is not an automatic thing; we must play our part in bringing it about. We may allow God to work our sufferings into His eternal plan and use them to bless others and to "complete" the sufferings of Christ, or, like the man in the parable who fell away when tribulations arose, we may be "offended" by them and thereby render them useless (Matt. 13:21 KJV). If God has entrusted us with suffering, let us set our hearts and minds to work together with Him to enable Him to bring out of our trials all the glory He longs us to know.

Nor is it only in eternity that God means us to share Christ's glory. Who has seen the radiance in the face of Joni Eareckson and not been conscious of God's glory then and there? God's desire for all His sufferers is that their very being may be filled to capacity with His glory even while they suffer. Nothing can more truly demonstrate the power and grace of God to men on earth and principalities and powers in the heavenly places than such a triumph.

Most of us have been awed at some time or another by a glimpse of God's glory in another's suffering; few of us have faced the fact that God wants to work a like miracle in our own. Let us lay our suffering before Him as a holy offering and ask Him to give through it all the blessing — even glory — that He means us to know!

· 30 ·

SUFFERING AND THE WILL OF GOD

A VERY HUMAN REACTION IN THE FACE OF UNEXPECTED suffering is to wonder if it is somehow the result of our having gotten out of favor with God. Should not things go well with us if we are walking in God's will? The Arch-Deceiver will work hard to persuade us that in some mysterious manner we must have strayed from God's will or we would not be experiencing this trouble. The Father of Lies knows well that if he can confuse us on this issue, he will succeed in robbing us of the confidence and peace with which God wants to sustain us in our suffering, and so he will hinder God's work in us and through us.

This lie is a powerful one because, like many of Satan's lies, it contains a half-truth: it is true that if we depart from God's will and wander in darkness, we will indeed know suffering. But this can happen only through conscious sin on our part, sin we refuse to confess and forsake; it can never come about without our knowledge and consent.

The remedy for such a situation lies in our own hands. When we turn to God in repentance and faith, He forgives us, cleanses us, and restores us to fellowship with Himself. Sometimes we may have to live with the results of such an experience — the course of our life may be changed as a result — but if we walk in fellowship with God thereafter, with no unconfessed and unforsaken sin between us, we walk in His will, and our trials are no reflection on our good standing with Him.

Although suffering is an intrusion into God's creation, and in this sense it is not God's will that His children should suffer, there remains a sense in which suffering may well be a part of God's will for our lives. Peter wrote of this in his letters to the

young churches in Asia. He warned them of the suffering that was
to be theirs and urged them not to be bewildered by it as if some
strange thing had happened to them; rather, he urged them to
rejoice because they were sharing Christ's sufferings and would also
share His glory (1 Pet. 4:12-13), and he went on to add words that
have blessed countless sufferers ever since: "Wherefore let them
that suffer according to the will of God commit the keeping of
their souls to him in well doing, as unto a faithful Creator"
(1 Pet. 4:19 KJV).

Our part in suffering in the will of God is twofold: first, we
are to commit the keeping of our souls to God, believing that He
is in control of our lives and trusting Him to do for us all that He
has promised. We must resist Satan's lies. We must not be deceived
into thinking that God "gave" us this suffering as a sadistic "gift"
because He wants us to suffer, that He is no longer in control in
our affairs, or that we have lost our way and strayed outside His
will. We must accept the fact that He has permitted this evil to
come to us, and we must commit its outcome, along with our
souls, into His keeping.

Second, we are to do this "in well doing": we are to concen-
trate on continuing to do the things that are well pleasing to God.
This means that we will witness a good confession in our suffering.
We will not fall apart when calamity strikes. It is not easy to
maintain a good witness in the face of sudden upset and pain, but
it is a part of our Christian responsibility. The spiritual confusion
and devastation we so often experience when suffering invades our
lives not only causes us needless pain but is a poor testimony to
others. It betrays a lack of spiritual maturity and shows that we do
not in fact possess the faith we profess.

Suffering borne with courage and confidence in God is a
powerful witness to His grace. Fear, anxiety, self-pity, and inner
havoc suggest to others that God is not all He claims to be, that
He is not sufficient for our needs. Many an observer has been
turned either towards God or away from Him by watching a Christian's response to suffering.

And not only other people, but a host of spiritual beings are
watching us as we suffer. God's honor is on trial before the principalities and powers in the sphere of spiritual reality. They watch
to see if God's life in us is able to triumph in our pain. Through

us, God is glorified or dishonored before heaven and hell. How we react to our suffering matters to our God.

The Creator into whose keeping we commit our souls and our suffering is faithful. He sealed His faithfulness to us with His own blood. No matter what suffering He may see fit to allow us, may we seek to be faithful to Him!

• 31 •

IT'S NO SIN TO BE SICK

AT ONE TIME OR ANOTHER IN OUR LIVES, MOST OF US EXPER-
ience some form of pain or illness. Perhaps that is why when we
think of suffering, we tend to pass over the other forms it may
take and think primarily of physical sickness. Thus, in the minds
of many, illness assumes a significance beyond its real importance.

In recent years a myth has grown up in Christian circles that
true Christianity should be accompanied by instant health. A distortion of biblical teaching, it is deceiving many believers and leaving a trail of destruction in its wake. Christians who are ill, especially
those suffering from a long-term illness, are thought by some to
be lacking in faith, out of God's favor, harboring secret sin, or
perhaps not Christians at all.

"Jesus wants you well" and "God is committed to your happiness" are themes that in some circles are superceding the biblical
call to repentance towards God, faith in the Lord Jesus Christ, and
obedience to the leadership of the Holy Spirit. Little heed is paid
to the overall teaching of the Scriptures concerning suffering. Usually only a few isolated verses are considered, and those not always
in context. Happiness seems to be more important than God's
standards of personal holiness.

Miracles are demanded to exorcise every pain. Those who
don't experience miracles are frequently looked upon with suspicion
by those who claim they do. International telecasts purvey the
Gospel of salvation plus instantaneous healing — or maybe even
forget about salvation and simply offer healing.

Meanwhile, those who have been led to expect a miracle are
shattered when it does not occur. Even more perilous is the state
of those whose conversion is predicated upon the hope of a healing
that does not follow. And who can measure the pressures put upon
sensitive believers who must live with continual suffering when

pastors, relatives, or friends do not hesitate to tell them that they suffer because of their own unbelief or secret sin?

What damage can be done by well-meaning Christians who take it upon themselves to "deal with" others about the "real reasons" for their illness! Such persons know little either about pain or the Scriptures. They grasp little of God's long-term purposes for His saints and fail to recognize His overruling sovereignty in the lives of His children. Consciously or unconsciously, they seem to equate their own good physical health with spiritual health, even superiority, and correct others accordingly. Many would utterly crumble under a small part of the suffering that their victim may be bearing with faith and fortitude. Yet they quickly saddle an already overborne soul with man-made guilt — a burden harder to bear than suffering itself. Only God can minister to the wounds inflicted by such cruelty. Only those who have experienced them can know their pain, and how long it takes them to heal.

Physical suffering, along with evils of every kind, is ours because of man's sin. Pain is no more God's will for man than is death; both are man's answer to God's gift of free will. Christians have no right to isolate illness and seek to exorcise it from our lives as if it were the ultimate evil. We are meant to war on all the wretched consequences of sin, not just one of them. To focus our efforts unduly on sickness is to ignore other evils equally if not more important.

Nowhere do the Scriptures promise God's children immunity from the suffering to which all mankind is heir because of sin. Evils come upon Christians and non-Christians alike, and this includes pain. No one has the right to assert that another's suffering is the result of his inadequacy or sin. Yet such claims are all too common, as every long-term sufferer knows to his sorrow. What help is there for those who must endure such torment as well as their physical affliction?

If ours is a problem of long-term illness or pain, we must free ourselves from the shackles of those who tell us that it is our own fault that we are not healed. We must repudiate such teaching, difficult as that may be, for it is not found in the Word of God. We are responsible to God, not to other people. It's no sin to be sick. Thousands of God's saints suffer illness in the will of God.

What we need is spiritual strength to withstand our troubles. We must set ourselves to discover what the Scriptures really teach about suffering and seek to live by that truth. We must embrace the sovereignty of God and align ourselves with His purposes, painful and inscrutable though they may seem to be. We must shelter our souls in the strong name of the Lord, commit ourselves to His care, and learn to rest in His wisdom and love.

We must seek to know God Himself, not be content merely to know *about* Him. We must love and worship Him for what He is, not for any gift He may give — not even the gift of health. We must learn to use the power of God to triumph over the evil Satan seeks to work us through our illness. We must set our hearts to harvest from our pain all the good God wants us to know. We must cooperate with Him to enable Him to work His eternal gain through our apparent loss.

Such experience of God through physical suffering is not easy and is never automatic. But it is not impossible. Thousands of God's people have proved His resurrection life in such circumstances through the centuries; thousands are doing so today. And only those who have known Him thus can tell of the glory He gives, not only in the life to come, but here and now.

WHAT ABOUT MIRACLES?

THOSE WHOSE VIEW OF SUFFERING IS TRULY BIBLICAL ARE UN-
likely to have problems about healing. While I deplore those who
stress healing out of all proportion and lay the burden of "little
faith" on sufferers whom God has not seen fit to heal, I have no
quarrel with Christians who seek or practice healing in a biblical
manner. Any believer who has a physical problem should certainly
seek healing from God. But this is a different thing from making
healing the major focus of our life and importuning God day and
night to work a miracle on our behalf.

There is no question but that God both can and does heal.
This is clearly seen both in the Old Testament and the New. Many,
if not most, of the miracles recorded in Scripture have to do with
physical healing.

In general, however, biblical miracles constituted a part of
God's progressive revelation of Himself as He marked the beginning of a new era by significant signs and wonders and validated
His prophets and disciples. Thus we see God the Father in His
covenant care of the emerging nation of Israel through which He
was to give the world His Word and His promised Redeemer. We
see God the Son in the miracles of Jesus as He proclaimed His
Sonship and redemption by demonstrating His power over nature
and over sin, sickness, death, and evil. We see God the Holy Spirit
in the miracles of the early church as He authenticated the Gospel
preached by the apostles through whom He was later to give the
New Testament documents. Other than in these historic clusters,
however, recorded miracles seem to have been infrequent and to
have occurred in particularly special circumstances.

There has never been a time when God has not been the
author of miracles. We must remember, however, that today we
do not need the miraculous demonstrations of God's power as
biblical generations did, when the Scriptures had not yet been
given. God used miracles to reveal His nature to His people, and

to assure them of His presence with them and His power on their behalf. We, however, know what God is like; we have His supreme self-revelation in the Lord Jesus Christ. We know His transcendent presence in the person of His Holy Spirit. We have the crowning demonstration of His power in the historically witnessed resurrection of His Son. We have the written Word of God to light our way.

It is significant that most true miracles today are taking place in parts of the world where thousands who have not previously heard the Gospel are being swept into the kingdom, where teachers are few and the Scriptures are not available or known. God is revealing Himself to new believers, demonstrating His presence and power and authenticating His messengers and work as He did in biblical times. The gifts of the Spirit given at Pentecost have never been withdrawn; subject to God's sovereign choice, they are still operative today. This includes the gift of healing.

No suffering Christian should fail to seek healing from God. He should recognize, however, that God works today through medicine, surgery, psychiatry, counselling, nursing, and a variety of professionally administered therapies more often than He does by divine intervention. God is the source of all healing; we must allow Him to work by whatever means He may choose. Yet it is not impossible that even today He may choose to work through a miracle.

It is not wrong to pray for miracles. But it *is* wrong to insist upon our own will rather than God's, to deny that He has promised glory through suffering. We may not demand miracles of a sovereign God. Unfortunately, such demands are made in all too many Christian circles today.

By insisting that God must work miracles on our behalf, we deny Him His divine prerogative. We ignore the fact that He may have richer blessings, deeper lessons, higher truths to impart to us in suffering than even a miracle of healing could allow. Who are we to entreat God to do His work according to our plan? To press such claims is to risk spiritual peril. God may grant our shortsighted request but send leanness to our souls.

Better to leave the miracle with God. Better to place ourselves totally in His hands, willing to accept whatever He gives or withholds. Better to trust Him to work for us in His own way a weight of spiritual glory greater than anything we can ask or think. We will find Him faithful.

· 33 ·

SPIRITUAL WHOLENESS

GOD HAS NOT ALWAYS HEALED THOSE WHO HAVE CRIED TO Him for release from physical suffering, as the history of the Christian Church from New Testament times to the present clearly shows us.

Paul's "thorn in the flesh" is an example. Although the apostle besought his Lord three times to remove the affliction, God chose to let it remain and to give sustaining grace instead. By strengthening Paul to triumph over evil even in the midst of evil, God demonstrated the reality of His power in a practical and painful situation to which all of humanity can relate. God has often chosen to display His grace rather than to heal His saints, and this may be His choice in your illness as well.

In addition to occasionally withholding physical healing, God sometimes chooses not to deliver His children from other forms of suffering. How clearly we see this as we read His roll-call of faith-heroes in the eleventh chapter of Hebrews! Here the names of those whom God commended for their faith and delivered from their trials is followed by a list of unnamed but equally faith-filled and commended saints whom He did not deliver.

And we must remember that the Apostle Paul knew spiritual health in overflowing abundance despite his physical weakness. His wholeness has blessed untold generations of Christians, blesses us today, and will continue to bless God's people far into the future. To some extent something similar is doubtless true of the suffering saints listed in Hebrews. It may be true of sufferers today.

God has His own reasons for working miracles for His children as well as for withholding them. Every sufferer seeking healing or deliverance must be willing to accept God's answer to his request. And for many of God's choice servants, His answer is often No.

We tend to think of healing in terms of cure, and of deliv-

erance in terms of a happy resolution to a painful situation. If God
does not remove our physical problem, we feel He has refused to
heal us; if He does not release us from our difficult circumstances,
we feel He has refused to deliver us. Yet nothing could be further
from the truth. God thinks of healing in terms of wholeness, of
deliverance in terms of triumph over evil.

God longs to impart to all His children the gift of spiritual
wholeness. He is more willing to give it than most of us are to
receive it. Every Christian may rejoice in spiritual health, but perhaps those who suffer physical limitations stand in a preferred
position in this regard. Pain throws us back on God in a way that
health does not. Our own helplessness makes us willing to accept
God's terms and to lay hold of His strength; thereby we may come
to know His spiritual healing. And spiritual wholeness, as experience has taught true Christians everywhere, is of infinitely greater
worth than physical health or deliverance from other painful situations, precious indeed as these gifts may be.

The problems from which God's children cry to Him for
deliverance are as diverse as the people who experience them; we
cannot hope to consider all of them here. Physical illness, however,
comes to most of us at some time or another. Sickness is a slow
form of death, one of the signatures of our mortality. At some
point it is almost certain to force most Christians to consider the
possibility of divine healing, whether for ourselves or someone
close to us; or some of our friends will consider it for us. Perhaps
this is reason enough to look into the question here.

As we have already noted, God does not always heal His
suffering children, but He does want all His people to know the
spiritual wholeness Christ purchased for them. How can the physical sufferer realize the wholeness that God longs to give? There
are several steps to spiritual health.

First, God's healing power cannot flow into a life where there
is any conflict concerning His lordship. We must fully accept God's
sovereignty, not just over human affairs in general, but over every
detail of our own personal lives. This means that we must not
endlessly argue with God about our illness. We must accept it as
being in God's will for us at this time. We must commit everything
connected with it, including our future, to His love and care. We
must truly recognize God as the sovereign Lord of our lives.

Second, any cloud that may have arisen between our soul

and God, or between ourselves and another person, may be a cause of our illness or impede our recovery from it. We must ask God to search our hearts and see if there is any sin that may be unconfessed and unforgiven, whether conscious or unconscious. If the Holy Spirit brings anything to our attention, no matter how seemingly insignificant, we must deal with it instantly and mercilessly. Even a so-called "little sin" can block God's healing power. Anger, bitterness, resentment, the harboring of an unforgiving or vengeful spirit — such things can and often do cause or increase physical illness. Following confession and forgiveness, a cleansed heart and a renewed spirit can result in a healed body, and often does.

Third, in the strong name of our conquering Lord, we must repudiate anything that is of Satan in our illness and claim Christ's victory over the evil the Adversary is trying to work us through it. While submitting ourselves humbly to God and accepting what He has allowed to come to us, we must also strongly resist the devil and seek to destroy his works.

Fourth, we must search out what the Scriptures really teach about healing and pray for it in a biblical way, remembering that Jesus taught that we must put God's glory and the advancement of His kingdom before our own needs. We should not spend time and energy running from one healing meeting to another seeking a miracle, or from one doctor to another seeking a cure at any cost, nor should we feel that we must try every cure-all our well-meaning friends may press upon us. Rather, we must cultivate the quietness of spirit that only God can give, and rest our case with Him. We should do what we can to alleviate our distress, but always we should recognize that healing and cure are not synonymous, and that much as we should like to experience both, true healing is of greater value than cessation of illness or pain.

Fifth, we must seek to understand the part that faith plays in healing. Faith is a necessary ingredient of healing just as it is of salvation, but faith is not the means of either. It is God who does the work, not our faith. Healing, like salvation, is God's free gift of grace; faith in itself has nothing to do with God's work. God has promised to save all who come to Him in faith for salvation, but He has given no comparable promise for healing; He may heal one believing Christian and leave another to suffer for years. This is His sovereign prerogative; we must bow to His choice. If He does not see fit to heal us, we must not reproach ourselves nor allow others to charge us with lack of faith. The reason we have not been healed lies deep within the inscrutable sovereignty of God. One day we shall know as we are known and understand His purposes. Meanwhile, we walk by faith and rejoice in hope of the glory of God, exulting in the spiritual wholeness that He denies to none of His needy children.

And last, though not least in importance, we must not neglect to seek healing through medical means. Whether we do this at the onset of our illness or later matters less than the spirit in which we do it. We must recognize that all healing is of God and that medical healing is not of lesser significance than healing by direct divine intervention. We must be willing to accept the fact that God may choose to heal us through human means if He is to heal us at all, and so we should make use of the best medical services available and cooperate completely with our physicians. This does not mean running from doctor to doctor seeking one who will tell us what we want to hear or jumping at nostrums. And we should not hesitate to use psychiatric or counselling services if they are suggested.

In all this, however, we may not demand that God heal us, either by medicine or by miracle. To do so is to declare, in effect, that we are unwilling to accept His sovereignty over our lives. If we want to experience God's wholeness, we must totally accept His choices for us, whatever they may prove to be.

Perhaps you have honestly met God's conditions for healing, and yet your illness persists. You may even know that it will be with you always. Rest assured that all the fullness of the Godhead stands ready to meet the need of the sufferer who, having not been granted physical healing, nevertheless asks from God the grace of spiritual wholeness in humility, love, and trust. Those who seek to know their God in this way shall not be disappointed.

• 34 •

GOD'S ALCHEMY

THROUGHOUT THE MIDDLE AGES, PATIENT SCHOLARS SPENT long years in the study of alchemy seeking a way to turn base metals into gold. Today we smile at their futile hopes. We know that man can never hope through alchemy to transform the common stuff of life into something precious. The only true alchemist is God. He has practiced His transmutation of evil into good from the beginning of time. God's alchemy is well documented in the Scriptures, and in the experience of multitudes of His children from biblical times right into the present.

Joseph is a classic biblical example. Sold into slavery by jealous brothers, unjustly imprisoned for a wrong he never did, seemingly forgotten by God and man, Joseph was nonetheless God's chosen instrument to preserve His people through years of famine that would otherwise have destroyed them. His suffering was transmuted by God into the salvation of Israel, through whom God was to bless the world in His gifts of the Savior and the Scriptures. "God sent me ahead of you . . . to save your lives," Joseph told his trembling brothers later. "It was not you who sent me here, but God. . . . You intended to harm me, but God intended it for good" (Gen. 45:7, 8, 50:20).

These words of faith have been claimed and found true by suffering believers ever since. What we experience as evil, God is turning into good. How often we have come to thank God for some evil that has befallen us, for we have found that through it God has given us clearer insights into His purposes and truth and imparted a knowledge of Himself that is precious beyond telling. So we, through patience and comfort of the Scriptures, have found hope (Rom. 15:4).

If we gave more serious heed to what the Scriptures teach about suffering being part of Christian discipleship, we would save ourselves much personal anguish and glorify God more truly in our lives. God is not the author of confusion, but of peace. If we are thrown into spiritual confusion when calamities overtake us, we will not glorify God before others nor experience His alchemy ourselves.

God cannot work out His design for our lives without our active cooperation, nor transmute Satan's evil into good for us unless we allow Him to do so. How can we learn to work with God to permit Him to perfect His purposes in us and for us? We must acknowledge His attributes — holiness, justice, righteousness, wisdom, love, faithfulness, goodness, sovereignty — and bow before Him in humble dependence as creatures before their Creator. We must accept His will for our lives, know with all our being that it is good, and trust Him to fulfill it. We must fully believe that He is able to accomplish His purposes for us in any circumstances and then rest in Him, resolutely refusing to consider other causes for our trouble.

This means that when suffering comes to us, whether physical, mental, spiritual, or circumstantial, we will not give way to fear and upset. Fear may well grip our hearts, to be sure, but it need not master us if we trust our God to keep His word to us. Satan may cause us hurt, but he cannot ultimately harm us, for God is in control.

We must learn to accept our suffering as coming from God. We must bring it to Him in faith, telling Him that we love and trust Him. We must claim His promise that He will overcome our evil with His good, even in this present painful situation. We must thank Him for His wisdom and His love and for the certainty of His sovereignty in the affairs of men and in our own personal lives. And as we thus learn to work together with our God, we will find that He is working His holy alchemy in our hearts and lives to fulfill His eternal purposes for us.

• 35 •

WHAT DO THE PROMISES MEAN?

Every suffering christian cries out to god in his pain, and rightly so. To whom but his Creator shall the creature turn for help in time of trouble? God has not only encouraged but commanded His people to call on Him in their distress. He has pledged in His Word to hear and answer our prayers. He has covered our every human exigency with a multitude of strong, specific promises which He has sworn He will fulfill. The pages of Scripture abound with shining records of a sovereign God meeting the necessities of His praying people. We are right to bring God's promises to His remembrance when we have special needs.

Yet in both the biblical record and our own experience, we find that God does not always answer in accordance with the promises pleaded before Him. Deliverance does not always come. Disaster is not always averted. We are not always healed of our diseases. Despite our most fervent prayers, our loved ones sicken and suffer and die. The Scriptures on which we have taken our stand sometimes seem to fail us. Our anguished hearts cannot help but ask the human question, "Why?"

What do God's promises mean? For an answer, we must look at the whole question of prayer.

Paul tells us that all God's promises, whether Old Testament or New, meet in the Person of Jesus Christ: "For no matter how many promises God has made, they are 'Yes' in Christ. And so through him the 'Amen' is spoken by us to the glory of God" (2 Cor. 1:20). Jesus' attitude towards prayer, then, and towards God's promises, must hold deep significance for His people.

In the New Testament we learn something of Jesus' thinking about prayer, and are permitted to observe Him, even listen in on Him, as He prays. His attitude towards prayer may be summed up in three passages of Scripture, two in the Gospels and one in the book of Hebrews. In the first two of these we see Jesus praying in the shadow of His cross. The human Son of Man shrank from the physical agony of crucifixion that was facing Him; the sinless Son of God recoiled in horror from the greater agony of separation from His Father that He had to undergo in order to become the Savior of sinful man.

Yet what was Jesus' prayer? In Matthew 26:39-44 we read that He three times besought the Father to deliver Him from the cross if that were possible, and three times declared His willingness to accept God's will rather than His own if deliverance could not be granted. In the more extensive record given in John 17, we read that He prayed for God's glory — that the Father would glorify, or reveal Himself in, His Son in order that the Son might glorify, or reveal, the true nature of God to mankind. He prayed for His disciples, who were even then sleeping despite His longing for the comfort of their presence in His anguish. He prayed for all those who would later come to believe on His name through their witness — which includes us, along with the believers of all other times and places. He remitted to His Father His completed earthly work, and then He went out to embrace the cross — to be made sin for us, and to endure the awful dereliction that that entailed.

In commenting on Christ's passion, the author of the epistle to the Hebrews states that when Jesus "offered up prayers and petitions with loud cries and tears to the one who could save Him from death," His prayers were indeed heard; nevertheless, despite His being God's beloved Son, He had to learn obedience by suffering in order to become the Author of our salvation (Heb. 5:7-9). In offering His will to God and enduring the cross rather than finding deliverance from it, Christ qualified as a merciful and faithful high priest for His people. His willingness to be made perfect through suffering has made prayer possible for us today.

It is likely that in praying to be delivered from the cross, Jesus would have contemplated some of the Old Testament promises concerning deliverance. Perhaps He even pleaded some of them before His Father. Was God unfaithful to His Word in allowing Jesus to proceed, unreprieved, to His crucifixion? Stop and think a moment. What was God's earliest promise to fallen man? Was it not the promise of ultimate deliverance from the power and penalty of the sin Adam and Eve had brought into the world? The woman's seed was to crush the serpent's head, but in so doing He would suffer a bruise Himself (Gen. 3:15).

When God in Christ was reconciling the world unto Himself on Calvary, He was not breaking His promise to mankind, but keeping it. He was fulfilling His covenant with Abraham, that in him all families of the earth should be blessed. He was keeping His covenant with David, that from his descendants should arise a King whose kingdom of justice and peace should know no end. In seeming to disregard certain immediate promises, God was bringing to pass other universal, ultimate, and infinitely richer promises and fulfilling His Word to restore sinful man to fellowship with Himself. In allowing His Son to die for the sins of the world, He was making possible the adoption of such sinners as you and I as sons and daughters of His own family. God was not breaking His promises; He was accomplishing them.

And Jesus recognized this in His prayer. In undergirding His petitions for deliverance with the submission of His own desires to His Father's will, He was acknowledging that God's consummation of His promise of redemption would preclude the fulfillment of any immediate promise of deliverance for Himself.

Sometimes this is so with God's Word to you and me today. Our immediate needs are so pressing that we feel nothing but deliverance from our present evil can fulfill God's promises to us. Often God does grant relief to His children; but all too often — perhaps more often than not — we do not experience such deliverance. Shall we not trust that even as our Father withholds the answer we desire to some present need, He is fulfilling His highest promise to us — His purpose to make us like Jesus Christ?

God's ways are not our ways. He sees the end from the beginning. His eyes are fixed on the ultimate fulfillment of His Word to His children. He purposes to present us faultless before the presence of His glory with an exceeding joy in which we shall rejoice in His presence forever. When He declines to grant us some immediate good, He is working through our suffering to bring His promised purpose to fruition. He has destined us for glory.

As we learn to lose our own desires in God's vast, all-wise and all-loving design, we come to know true peace. We are enabled to see our mild afflictions — those things that seem to us so overwhelming — in their eternal perspective: they are part of God's plan for perfecting us in Christ's likeness. And with Frances Havergal and untold thousands who have proved God's faithfulness, we come to know the truth of the song we sometimes heedlessly sing:

> We may trust Him fully
> All for us to do;
> They who trust Him wholly
> Find Him wholly true.

• 36 •

PRAYING IN JESUS' NAME

WHAT DOES IT MEAN TO PRAY IN JESUS' NAME? IN OLD TEStament times, prayer was offered only in the context of sacrifice. God's people brought an offering when they came into His presence: it cost them something to draw near to God. As they called on His name, they offered Him not only their visible sacrifices, but with it, the sacrifice of their hearts and lives and wills. When Jesus lived on earth, He took part in the services of the synagogue and prayed according to the Old Testament pattern. Underlying all His recorded private prayers we see the Old Testament principle of sacrifice, and we see this pattern repeated throughout the prayers of the New Testament. If we want to pray the kind of prayers that He can hear and answer, we too must pray in the spirit of sacrifice. What does this mean for us?

Jesus taught His followers to pray to the Father *in His name*. In biblical usage, the name of God is synonymous with His person and being. He revealed different facets of His character to His people in various situations by the use of different names. Thus we have *Elohim:* God the mighty Creator and governor of all things; *Jehovah:* God the Lord, the eternal, self-existent God of righteousness, holiness, and love; *El-Shaddai:* God the almighty, who nourishes and sustains; *Adonai:* God the Lord and master of His people; *Jehovah-Jireh:* the God who provides; *Jehovah-Rophe:* the God who heals; *Jehovah-Nissi:* the Lord my banner; *Jehovah-Tsidkenu:* the Lord our righteousness; *Jehovah-Shalom:* the God who is our peace; *Jehovah-M'Kaddesh:* the Lord our Sanctifier; *Jehovah-Rohi:* the Lord my shepherd; *Jehovah-Shammah:* the God who is always there; and the Christmas name of God, *Jehovah-Jesus:* the Lord our Savior. God's people came to know God's nature in His names; God's character and God's name are one.

If we are to pray in Jesus' name, then, we must pray in His character — pray as He prayed. Jesus' prayers focused on the Fa-

ther's will rather than on His own desires. If we would pray as He
prayed, we, too, must submit ourselves to God. It is not in the
nature of fallen man to pray so selflessly. Indeed, unless God takes
the initiative, it is not in our nature to pray at all. By nature we
turn each one to our own way, not God's. If man prays, it is
because God has already touched him and turned his wayward
spirit towards Himself. But God *has* taken this initiative. He has
not merely commanded us to pray, He has made it possible for us
to pray. He has put His Spirit within us, the Spirit who makes us
His sons and enables us to look up to Him in love and trust and
cry, "*Abba,* Father!" (Rom. 8:15).

Paul teaches that it is by "the promised Holy Spirit," who
is the guarantor of our salvation, that we have been sealed into
Christ (Eph. 1:13-14). The Spirit helps us in our weaknesses, particularly our weakness in prayer, and "intercedes for us . . . in accordance with God's will" (Rom. 8:26-27). Who better can teach the
suffering Christian to discern God's promises and to plead them
in Jesus' name than He who is Himself the Holy Spirit of promise?
He alone can mediate God's promises to us so that we understand
them correctly and trust God to work them out for our highest
good. We bring His Word to Him in faith, knowing that in one
way or another He will fulfill it, for it cannot return to Him void—
it must accomplish His purpose.

But we must pray in Jesus' name. We must offer our own
desires to God in spiritual sacrifice. We must leave Him free to
bring His promises to fruition for us either in the immediate realm
of the physical or the ultimate realm of the spiritual. At one time
He may touch us in both areas of life; at another He may extend
spiritual healing or deliverance only. If this is His choice, we must
take care not to hinder Him from revealing to us the wealth of
spiritual riches He longs to have us discover in the answer He has
given.

God could have chosen to run His universe without involving
Himself in the prayers of His people or engaging them in His
purposes, but that has not been His choice. Rather, He has appointed our prayers to be the lever that releases His power and
enables Him to keep His promises to us and to accomplish His
will for us and in us.

In His sovereignty and grace He has invited—even commanded—us to come to Him in prayer. He has given us great and

precious promises to present before Him. He has given us His Spirit to teach us to pray, and to pray in us and for us and with us. Ceaselessly He listens to the intercessions that our great high priest is making before His throne on our behalf. And to this holy stream of prayer He bids His children add the feeble trickle of our own petition, urging us to come boldly before Him to obtain mercy for our weaknesses and find grace to help in our time of need. He asks only that we pray in Jesus' name.

Origen held that prayer is not primarily a matter of petition but of participation in the life of God. How could we learn to share God's life — essentially an *eternal* blessing — if He granted our every request for *temporal* good? When we truly seek the Father's face in Jesus' name in the context of the spiritual sacrifice of our will to God's, we shall find that we may safely leave the outcome of our requests for our temporal necessities in His hands.

Recently I was told the story of a tiny child who wanted to help his father garden. The father knew that there was nothing the toddler could do to help him, but he loved to involve his little son in his activities. Loading the wheelbarrow with earth, he invited the youngster to reach up and take hold of its handles. Then, placing his own strong hands over the little one's weak ones, he "helped" him to push the barrow to the flower bed he was preparing. Although the child's fragile strength could contribute nothing to the task, he grew in spirit and in oneness with his father as he shared his activity and participated in his life.

And so it is with God's children. As we come to God in Jesus' name, praying as He prayed, our wills in submission to His, God lets us place our puny hands on His great purposes — purposes too lofty for our finite minds to comprehend — and participate in carrying out His plan. Graciously covering our feeble prayers with His sovereignty, He pushes the barrow where He will until His purpose is accomplished.

We must accept His choice. We may not always understand His workings, and our problems may not always be resolved as we had hoped, but slowly we will come to recognize that at the deepest levels of our being, God's promises to us are indeed being fulfilled. By sharing in His life, we will find our truest destiny and experience the highest joy the human spirit is capable of knowing.

• 37 •

PUTTING FAITH TO WORK

YOU HAVE PROBABLY BEEN READING THESE PAGES BECAUSE YOU are seeking answers to some overwhelming personal sorrow. You may have been struggling with it for years. Possibly you have considered your situation hopeless. But you are a Christian. You know and love God. As you have pondered the biblical teachings about suffering, perhaps you have glimpsed a ray of light in your darkness. Now you long to experience its full radiance, to live in its hope. You have come to realize, maybe for the first time, that your life, no matter how circumscribed it may be, is held in the hands of the God who is sovereign not only in His universe, but in everything that concerns you personally. You have discovered that your suffering, far from being the senseless waste it may seem, is pregnant with eternal significance — that through it God wants to work for you what Paul calls an "eternal weight of glory" (2 Cor. 4:17 KJV). Now you want to experience God in a new way, to prove the power of His sovereignty in your pain. What practical steps can you take to touch your personal sorrow with the glory of the sovereignty of God?

Although individual circumstances may call for slightly differing approaches to this question, all sufferers have one common starting point: we must return again and again to the great foundational truths of Scripture concerning human suffering. We have considered these in some detail in the preceding pages, but even at the risk of appearing repetitive, we must review and summarize them here. Our suffering is continually reasserting its presence; if we would triumph over Satan's power in our pain, we must continually reassert the facts of God's mighty responses to his evil. As Jesus countered Satan's every attack with His quiet "It is written," so, too, must we. We cannot repeat God's truths to ourselves too frequently; we gain ascendency over the Evil One with each repetition.

Here, then, is a recapitulation of the four basic truths on which we stand — our stepping stones to freedom:

First, we must recognize with absolute certainty that God is in control in His universe. He is sovereign over evil, sin, death. Though for His own inscrutable reasons God has allowed Satan certain temporary powers, the Evil One holds them only under God's sovereignty. Satan's powers may be great, but they are limited both in intensity and in duration. So far may he go in his wicked intent against God's people, but no farther. He may hurt us, but he cannot ultimately harm us. The ultimate triumph is God's, and ours in Him. Consciously and deliberately we must make this glorious truth the personal foundation-stone of our faith.

Second, we must accept the fact that we live in a fallen world and that God has not promised His people immunity from the suffering that is the common heritage of our fallen humanity. We are sinful men and women, and the wages of sin is death. Our sufferings are simply the slow outworking of the death sentence that mankind has passed on himself by his sin. Christian and non-Christian alike, all must share in one way or another in the pain of the universe. We must accept the portion of suffering that comes to us knowing that however severe it may be it is still less than sinful creatures deserve from a righteous God.

But we do not forget that, sinners though we are, God has made us His children through faith in Jesus Christ. We do not suffer in darkness, but in hope. Despite the evil our powerful Adversary seeks to work us in his efforts to strike back at his mighty conqueror, God is still quietly pursuing His purposes for His children. Satan's evil cannot negate God's sovereignty; our Father works through all things, even our pain, for our eternal good. He is using the sufferings by which Satan seeks to undo us to re-create us in His holy image — that image in which He created us originally, but which we shattered by our sin. Through all that happens to us in this life, God is perfecting His purpose of glorifying us — of gradually, by His Spirit, making us like Jesus Christ.

Third, we must recognize that we live in a world of spiritual warfare, a warfare in which Satan, with all the powers at His command, ceaselessly seeks to destroy God's kingdom, a warfare in which God's children themselves are the battlefield. Not only must Christians accept their share of the pain of the universe, but because they are part of God's kingdom — and particularly if they are faithfully seeking to extend it — they must also expect to experience all the hostility of hell. We must consciously acknowledge, accept, and seek to understand these uncomfortable but very real facts of the Christian life if we hope to learn to triumph in the spiritual conflict which will be ours as long as we live. The ultimate victory is Christ's and so ours, but we must do constant combat with a strong and ruthless foe.

And fourth, in the light of these biblical truths, we must truly accept whatever sorrows God allows to enter our lives, trusting Him to work through Satan's evils for our highest good. God is not the author of our suffering; pain is Satanic in origin. But it comes to us only under God's control, and He uses it to fulfill His purposes for us and in us. One day He will banish all evil forever from His universe. But until then, suffering will continue to be a part of human life and God's children are not exempt. We must accept our pain as from His hand and see that we do not hinder Him from bringing His purposes to fruition through it.

As was pointed out earlier, this does not mean that we will not do everything in our power to alleviate our pain. We will draw on all the resources at our command, both temporal and spiritual, to help us. We will bring God's promises to Him in believing prayer. If our problem is a physical one, we will fulfill every scriptural injunction concerning healing, as well as make responsible use of such ethical forms of medical help as we may need, and leave the results with God. We will do everything possible to overthrow the evil that Satan sends into our lives.

But we will accept the fact that God may not answer our prayers in the way that we had hoped. We will recognize that He may choose to fulfill an ultimate rather than an immediate promise concerning our healing or deliverance. We will pray as Jesus prayed, offering our wills to God in living sacrifice. We will be willing to accept His answer, whatever it may be, and trust Him to work His will for us through it. We will seek to find the spiritual significance in what God allows to come into our lives and work with Him to perfect His purposes through it.

This, then, is the way in which God's people may learn to put their faith to work and find meaning and purpose in suffering. We must think, pray, and act from this biblical foundation, constantly clinging to the certainty of God's sovereignty. As we do this we shall find that on that sure basis faith will build a holy resting place where we may dwell content with God. There we shall know joy, hope, and spiritual service, no matter what our outward circumstances may be.

• 38 •

"SOVEREIGN LORD!"

LET'S GO ON NOW TO CONSIDER ANOTHER PRACTICAL STEP we can take toward discovering meaning and purpose in our personal sorrows, turning to the third and fourth chapters of the book of Acts.

Peter and John healed a congenital cripple at the entrance to the Temple in Jerusalem in the name of the Lord Jesus and then addressed the awe-struck crowd, proclaiming the power of the risen Christ; many people had come to believe in Him. The priests and rulers were upset and had the disciples jailed overnight. The next morning they were brought before the Sanhedrin, who forbade them under threat of punishment to teach or to speak further in Jesus' name. What did Peter and John do? They went back to their Christian friends, told them what had happened, and together they prayed. Luke records their prayer in Acts 4:24-30. It holds deep significance for suffering believers still.

What did the disciples pray for? Did they ask if they should continue to preach in Jesus' name? No, they knew they must proclaim Christ at any cost, no matter how strong the opposition might be. Rather than dwelling on the difficulties that faced them, they looked beyond their problems to the God who was sovereign over them. They asserted their confidence that God was greater than their storm. They affirmed their steadfast faith in the sovereignty of the God they knew and loved.

"Sovereign Lord!" they began. Then they praised God for His mighty power displayed in creation and His sovereign working in human history. They laid their situation before Him, and asked Him to enable them despite it to speak His Word with great boldness. They prayed that God would further glorify His Son by working more miraculous signs and wonders in His name, even though they knew that would bring the wrath of the authorities down upon them. And we read that after they had prayed, the place was shaken and they were all filled afresh with the Holy Spirit, and spoke the Word of God boldly.

This is what we must do in our own situations. By deliberate and definite acts of will, we must place our suffering under the sovereignty of God. We must tell Him that we love Him and trust Him, that we believe He is sovereign over our problems no matter how overwhelming they may be, and we must do this whether we feel it or not. We must search out the grounds of our faith both in the biblical record and in our own personal history, and present them to God. We must affirm our confidence in His being and character and our faith in His ability and willingness to govern our affairs in our best interest. We must bring His promises before Him, making sure always that we place each Scripture in its correct framework and do not seek to use it as some out-of-context proof text which God cannot honor. And always with our petitions we must bring the sacrifice of our wills to God's will, as Jesus did.

Such acts of will are not once-and-for-all experiences, although they must indeed have one particular starting point. They are commitments that will have to be made many times over, affirmations that must be renewed daily. We must constantly remind ourselves of the unchangeable certainty of God's sovereignty over all that concern us, and constantly tell Him of our faith in His wisdom and power to fulfill His purposes for us.

Such affirmations are not static; they will deepen and grow with the passing years, becoming more and more meaningful as we mature in our Christian lives. Our commitment, like the Christian life itself, must always be a living, moving force.

"Sovereign Lord!" As we come to God with these words on our lips and in our hearts, willing to accept what suffering may be ours and to honor Him in our pain, we enable God's Spirit to form Jesus Christ deep within us. Such prayer may or may not change our circumstances, but one thing is certain: it will slowly but surely change the people who pray it. The "way of escape" that God promised His people (1 Cor. 10:13 RJV) may prove for us to be nothing more than the ability to endure our trial, but is that so small a thing? As we allow God to do His work in us through our suffering, gradually He is changing us — glorifying us with the radiant image of the Son of God for whose glory we were created, and in whose glory alone we shall realize our true destiny.

• 39 •

NOT FEELINGS, BUT FACTS

THOUGH A CAREFUL STUDY OF WHAT THE SCRIPTURES TEACH about suffering may lead us to an intellectual acceptance of God's sovereignty over our suffering, can we ever hope to experience any sensible *feelings* that this is so? It is probably safe to say that few, if any, of us are likely to know such feelings. Most of us struggle with overwhelming feelings of anger, helplessness, and hopelessness if we are not sunk into depression. Some of us are so defeated by our feelings that we refuse even to consider our problem in the light of God's sovereignty and so rob ourselves of the good He longs to work us in our pain.

How comforting to know that in our battle with suffering we do not depend on human feelings, but on immutable facts — the sure and certain facts of God's eternal Word! A consciousness of God's sovereignty over pain is not something we have by nature, nor does it come to us ready made. It is something we ourselves have to develop. In this conflict, as in all else in the Christian life, we must learn to walk by faith, not by sight or feelings. And how can such faith be found? "Faith comes from hearing the message," Paul tells us in Romans 10:17, "and the message is heard through the Word of Christ."

It is when we give ourselves unremittingly to the contemplation of the Scriptures that the Holy Spirit is set free to kindle in our hearts the faith we need to deal with our problems and realize God's sovereignty over them. And when by deliberate acts of will we nurture that feeble flame until it glows brightly in our hearts, He implants within us a tiny seed of consciousness of God's sovereign working in our lives. Rooted in the Word of God, watered by the Spirit's dew, and warmed by our flickering faith, God's good seed begins to sprout. As by study of the Scriptures and by prayer we cultivate the tender plant, it leafs, buds, and blossoms. Finally it brings forth the fruit we need to sustain us in our suffering.

While it is God who gives the increase, and Him alone, it is also true that we reap the harvest we ourselves have sown. If we sow the wind we shall reap the whirlwind, and many do just that, suffering spiritual loss; but if we set ourselves to sow and nurture God's Word in our hearts continually, we shall surely reap the holy harvest He longs that we should know.

And this harvest is infinitely more than just the presence of sensible feelings that God is present in our pain. Such feelings may or may not be ours; eventually we shall discover that their presence or absence doesn't really matter. Gradually we shall find ourselves surprised by a dawning awareness of God Himself — an expanding sense of who and what He is, a growing understanding of His purpose, His power, His faithfulness, and His love.

Little by little, we shall learn to trust God where we can't understand Him. We shall experience an ever-deepening consciousness of His sovereignty in the affairs of His universe, and slowly we shall come to discern something of our own small place in His eternal plan. Our wavering feelings will be replaced by a profound certainty — the deep, settled assurance that our times are in God's hands and that He is well able to perfect His purposes for us, whether through our sufferings or despite them.

What can we do to help bring about this shift in our inner emphasis from feelings to facts? The only way I know is what I call the "over-and-over-again syndrome." This is simply laying hold of God's great foundational facts one by one and repeating them over and over again in His presence, regardless of our feelings. We tell God honestly that we have no sensible awareness that He is in control of our lives, but we believe it because He has said so. We confess our fears and doubts before Him one by one and repudiate them before the certainties of Scripture. Over and over again we bring before Him the same eternal verities — and often the same failures of unbelief — and affirm our faith in Him, taking our stand on His Word rather than our own feelings and failings.

We must do this consciously, deliberately, constantly, no matter what our outward situation may be. We must continue to do it day by day, hour by hour, even moment by moment, as long as we live. We must repeat before God again and again our dependence on the promises He has given us in His Word, and with John Newton we must affirm our belief that "He cannot have taught us to trust in His name, and thus far have brought us, to put us to shame!"

Gradually, as we make this over-and-over-again syndrome the relentless resolve of our inner life, we shall find our faith growing until it overshadows and finally overthrows our contrary feelings. One day we shall realize with joy and gratitude that the consciousness of God's sovereignty we had so longed to know has dawned upon us unawares. Its light will shine in our darkness, and though our suffering may not be less, we will be at peace.

• 40 •

THE GATEWAY OF PRAISE

ANOTHER AVENUE THROUGH WHICH WE MAY GROW IN OUR consciousness of God's sovereignty over our pain is that of praise. "You will call your walls Salvation and your gates Praise," wrote a long-ago prophet (Isa. 60:18); and praise is indeed a gateway through which we may rise to higher levels of Christian maturity. In the words of an anonymous singer,

> Praise is purer far
> Than any form of prayer:
> Prayer climbs the steep ascent to Heaven —
> Praise is already there.

In recent years much has been written about the power of praise, not all of it truly biblical. There are those who insist that we can't hope to experience God's deliverance in our pain until we thank Him for it. "You've got to thank Him for it," they belabor their suffering friends, thereby increasing their pain rather than alleviating it.

If we think this idea through, we will realize that to thank God for pain — which is one slow form of the death that is ours because of sin — is really to thank God for sin itself. This is something no Christian can rightly do. Yet praise, correctly understood and consciously put to work, is indeed a powerful weapon in the hands of a suffering Christian.

No, we must not thank God for our pain: it is evil and comes to us from Satan. But we must recognize that God has allowed it to enter our lives and that He is sovereign over it, and we must accept our suffering as from His hand. In His name we must repudiate the evil that Satan hopes to inflict upon us through it, and we must praise God for His power to restrain that evil and to work through it for our good.

When we have this biblical pattern firmly fixed in our minds, we are in a position to put the power of praise to work to help us in our suffering. How do we go about this? Basically, we must praise God for Himself, for what He is, for His nature and being, and we must do this by a deliberate act of will. The Scriptures resound with the affirmations of God's people, many of them in deep difficulties, who set themselves by decisive acts of will to praise their God. Listen to the psalmists: "Thou art my God, and I will praise thee: thou art my God, I will exalt thee" (Psa. 118:28 KJV). "I will praise your name, O Lord, for it is good" (54:6). "I will always have hope; I will praise you more and more" (71:14). "Because your love is better than life, my lips will glorify you" (63:3). We, too, must set our hearts to praise our God.

When we begin to praise God for what He is, we will find endless vistas opening before us. As we contemplate His attributes one by one and consider their meaning for ourselves in our particular situation, our hearts cannot but be drawn towards God in wonder and gratitude and praise. Praise for God's majesty, His holiness, His righteousness; praise for His wisdom, His justice, His power; praise for His faithfulness, His goodness, His truth; praise for His love, His mercy, His grace — shall we ever be able to plumb the depths of the fountainhead of praise that is our God?

We must let our imagination go, and consider what God in all His multifaceted being really means to us — not academically, but in practical fact. We should try to envisage what our life would be without Him, without the assurance of His love, His comfort, His provision for our needs. We might imagine having to bear our burdens alone, with no recourse to prayer, no Scriptures to encourage us, no Christian fellowship to support us. Should we give ourselves seriously to such contemplation, we might begin to realize, perhaps for the first time, something of what God really does mean to us, and our hearts will be drawn out to Him in fervent praise. We must worship Him in wonder and in awe, and bow before His sovereignty and grace.

Does this perhaps seem to you to be too cerebral an exercise to kindle your soul to praise? Do you feel it is too difficult an undertaking in view of your present suffering? It can begin very simply. As we read the Scriptures each day, we can ask God to reveal Himself to us and to speak to our particular need. One day the Holy Spirit will quietly touch a familiar word with a new radiance. We will catch a glimmer of new meaning concerning some aspect of God's nature or dealings with His people. Suppose the word is *faithfulness*. We can let the Spirit's gentle promptings pass, or we can stop and ask Him to teach us more about God's faithfulness and its meaning for us in our need. We can do this by a small but conscious act of will.

We can pause and recall other Scripture verses about faithfulness, perhaps jotting down a few thoughts or references. We can recollect a few lines of a hymn about God's faithfulness, look them up, sing them, or even memorize them.

We can think back to times in biblical history when God showed Himself faithful to His covenant people. We can recall times in our own lives when we, too, found Him faithful to His Word. Other memories will crowd into our consciousness as we reflect on His faithfulness in our circle of family and friends. A surge of gratitude greater than we have ever known will sweep over us. We will find ourselves praising God deeply and truly for His faithfulness to all who trust Him, and we will commit ourselves and our problems afresh to His faithful care.

We may stop here for the time being, or we may go on. We may take our concordance and turn to the word *faithfulness*. As we look up the references, suddenly we will find ourselves awed and overwhelmed. God's faithfulness will take on new and personal meaning for us, and our hearts will be overflowing with wonder and thanksgiving. And as we praise God for His faithfulness, how can we help but go on to His sovereignty? We will bow before Him in praise and adoration, and our sufferings will fall into their proper perspective before our faithful and sovereign Lord.

And so, as word by word we contemplate God's attributes, little by little we will grow in our knowledge and understanding of who and what He is. And we will find that understanding leads onwards to praise, and praise leads onwards to perspective, and perspective leads onwards to power over the evils with which Satan seeks to harm us. Slowly but surely we will learn to live in the light of God's sovereignty and to use His spiritual armor to triumph over our spiritual foes.

•41•

PARADOX

FOR FORTY YEARS I WAS PRIVILEGED TO SPEND MY SUMMERS in a beloved wilderness retreat in northern Ontario, where I lived with delight on the rocky shores of the Severn River. I rejoiced in the shining sweep of its waters in all their moods and never tired of watching its ever-changing vistas. Many times I reflected on a paradox I witnessed there.

The river had its source in Lake Simcoe, twenty-six miles to the southeast. Its waters moved through Lake Couchiching and Sparrow Lake, then flowed west for another twenty-six miles, dropping slowly through a series of locks to lose themselves in Georgian Bay before finding their way through the Great Lakes and the St. Lawrence River down to the ocean.

Although the Severn flowed westwards, its waters usually appeared to be moving to the east. The prevailing winds in that region were westerly. Blowing in from Lake Huron, they were funnelled upstream between the massive rocks that guarded the deep river valley, sweeping the waters in sparkling white-crowned wavelets eastwards before them. Only in the pre-dawn stillness of certain windless mornings could the careful watcher discern that far below, the current was flowing strongly and steadily westwards and onwards to the sea.

This sort of apparent contradiction between appearance and reality is characteristic of the Christian life in many ways, too, particularly for those who must suffer. The Apostle Paul gives two lists of this sort of paradox in his second letter to the Corinthians. In the first passage (2 Cor. 4:6-18), he gives us a beautiful and familiar statement concerning our Christian identity and calling, telling us that God, who called light to shine out of darkness, has shone in our hearts to make known to us, and through us to others, His glory in Jesus Christ. He goes on to say that God has hidden this treasure "in jars of clay" — committed it to people such as you

123

and I — so that everyone must recognize that the power at work in us is not human power, but God's power. He then illustrates the meaning of this for the Christian by setting forth a series of striking paradoxes that cannot but sound a responsive chord in the heart of every suffering believer.

Christians, says Paul, are troubled on every side, yet they are not distressed. They are perplexed, but they are not in despair. Though they are persecuted, they are not forsaken; though they are cast down, they are not destroyed. In their innermost being, they will experience Christ's death, yet to others they will show forth Christ's life. Though the outward man may be perishing, every day the inward man is being renewed. Though they are suffering a short-term, light affliction now, they will reap an eternal and exceedingly great weight of glory as a result.

Paul tells us how to stand up to such a life. He exhorts us not to focus our attention on the things that are visible and temporal — things as they seem to be now — but rather to fix our eyes and hearts on the things that are invisible and eternal — things as they really are. He urges us to learn to look at our lives from God's perspective, and so to live in triumph over our present suffering. As we are able to do this, Christ's life and Christ's glory will be made known through us to others.

Paul's second statement is found in 2 Corinthians 6. In the first part of the chapter he encourages his friends to be faithful in their sufferings and to live lives worthy of their high calling as Christ's servants. Then in verses 9-10 he continues with his paradoxes: Christians, he says, are unknown and yet well known — though men may pay little attention to us, every one of us is well known to God. Though we may seem to be dying, yet we live with the very life of God Himself. We are chastened, but we are not killed. Though we are sorrowful because of our sufferings, yet always in the depths of our being we are rejoicing with unspeakable joy. We are poor in the sight of others, yet we make many rich as we share with them the abundance of God's grace. Of ourselves we have absolutely nothing, but in Jesus Christ there is nothing that we do not possess.

Do you find it hard to realize God's sovereignty in your pain? Do you feel that the waters of your life are moving away from your desired haven rather than towards it? Think deeply on Paul's paradoxes.

All through the Scriptures we are taught that suffering and glory are inextricably bound up with one another. God has never promised that our lives will be free from suffering, but rather that He will be with us in our pain and will not only sustain us in it but will actually work through it to bring about that destiny of glory for which He created us — to make us like His Son.

Even Jesus had to pass through suffering to glory, had to endure the cross in order to reach the joy that was set before Him. That joy was His glory — and ours — the joy of bringing you and me home to His Father's house as sons and daughters of God, each one of us perfect and like Him at last, shining with His glory forever.

God's sovereign power and love are at work in your life as surely as my river's current flows to the ocean despite the appearance of its surface waters. Look away from the temporal to the eternal, from the visible to the invisible, from things as they seem to be to things as they really are. In the sovereign sweep of the resistless current of the mighty Spirit of God, the waters of your life are slowly but surely moving homewards to their source.

• 42 •

FIVE GOLD RINGS

WE BEGAN OUR STUDY BY CONSIDERING THE PERFECT PLAN that the three persons of the Godhead formed for man in eternity before they laid the foundations of the earth. We have traced, however dimly, something of the outworking of that plan in time and history. We have sought to see its significance for suffering humanity, and to find its meaning for our own lives, especially with reference to the problems of pain and evil we all encounter. We have found that the New Testament teaches that suffering is an integral part of the lives of God's children as it was for Christ, evidence of the fact that we shall one day enter into the fullness of the glory for which God has destined us. Suffering, a stumbling block to faith in Old Testament times, is seen in the New Testament as a basic ingredient in the perfecting of God's purposes for His people. Though suffering is the devil's intrusion, God is using it to transform sinful men and women into the likeness of His holy Son. We draw our studies to a close by reflecting for a time on the sure and certain hope that is ours in Christ.

Nowhere has God given us a more radiant vision of His destiny for His children, and His power to carry it out, than in the closing verses of the eighth chapter of Romans. In that passage (vv. 28-39) God, through His apostle Paul, assures His people of His power to secure them from evil and to perfect His purposes for them. Through all the circumstances and events of our lives, He tells us, He is working for His glory and our good. He is working Satan's evils into His holy design, transmuting them into everlasting glory. He affirms that, by this sovereign working, all those who have been called according to His purpose shall know that purpose fulfilled (v. 28). As pledge that this will be so, God has surrounded His children with a chain of five gold rings, eternally interlocking, inviolable as God Himself, each a sure word of promise that cannot be broken. Within the golden circle of His everlasting covenant, God's people dwell secure, unthreatened by the evils Satan seeks to work them. Their souls are safe, no matter what their suffering, for nothing can penetrate God's fortress but what His love permits. Stronger than the powers of death and hell abides the living Word of God.

We find the words of God's impregnable circle of promises in verses 29 and 30: God's children have been *foreknown, predestined, called, justified,* and *glorified.* These shining truths embrace the whole purpose of God from eternity past, through time, and on to eternity yet to come. The first two took place before time began; the next two are taking place now; the last one, though begun in time and still going on, will only be consummated at Christ's coming.

Foreknown signifies God's thought for us in eternity. In His creative mind He envisaged a family of men and women upon whom He could shower the abundance of His love and favor. He considered us and resolved to create us and make us His children. Long before God called us into existence, He knew us for His own.

Predestined means that having come to a decision about us, God ordained that His purpose should be implemented: "he chose us in him before the creation of the world to be holy and blameless in his sight. In love he predestined us to be adopted as sons through Jesus Christ" (Eph. 1:4-5). And so, in the eternally distant past, God both knew us and chose us to be His; and He had the power to carry out His purpose.

Then God moved into the realm of time and *called* us to Himself. One by one we heard His voice in the innermost depths of our being. One by one, no two in quite the same way, we responded in faith to His compelling call, believed on His name, and became His children. We were born into God's family and sealed as His sons by His Holy Spirit. Nothing in earth or hell can ever abrogate our heavenly calling — God's historical outworking of His eternal predestination to adopt us as His children — nor can we do so ourselves. No matter what ills may overtake us in our journey from earth to heaven, we are God's called ones, His own.

And those whom God called He also *justified.* He has declared us righteous for Jesus' sake and accepted us in Him. He has forgiven our sin — not only the sins we have committed, past, present, and future, but the basic sin of what we are by nature, our state of rebellion against Himself. Neither our own conscience nor earthly foe nor fiend of hell can now accuse us, for God sees us as we appear before Him in Christ Jesus, clothed in His righteousness, righteous as He is righteous. I stand in Christ "just as if I'd" never sinned at all — justified in Him.

God's act of justification, though conclusive and eternal, is not an end in itself. Rather, it is the initiation into our life as God's children. We shall spend the rest of our lives working it out — learning by the power of the Holy Spirit to live the lives of holiness for which God has foreknown, predestined, called, and justified us. We shall often fail. But God will never cease working to form Christ's image in us; He begins on earth the work of glory that will only be completed in eternity. And even our failures cannot nullify the strength and reality of this shining ring in God's gold circle of security. "By grace alone, through faith alone in Christ alone," as has been written, always and forever we have been, and are, *justified.*

And "those he justified, he also *glorified*" — thus God completes the protective circle of His five gold rings. The plan that He purposed in eternity He will bring to perfection in eternity. "How great is the love the Father has lavished on us, that we should be called children of God!" marvels John. "And that is what we are! . . . now we are children of God, and what we will be has not yet been made known. But we know that when he appears, we shall be like him, for we shall see him as he is" (1 John 3:1-2). What manner of love, indeed, has the Father bestowed on us, that poor, guilty sinners as we are, the sons of ignorance and night, we should one day shine with the purity and perfection of His Son Jesus Christ! *This* is the glory for which God has destined us, that we should become like Jesus and live with Him forever.

God is using everything that happens to us in this life to prepare us for this glorious destiny. He is using our sufferings to make us like Jesus, gradually changing us into His likeness from one degree of glory to another until finally, His work completed, we shall bear His image forever. And this work is going on today. God began to glorify us — to create His own nature in us by His Spirit — the day He justified us and sealed us as His. As long as we live He will continue His work of glorifying us until we appear perfected in His presence. And so certain is He of His ability to finish the work He has begun that He sees it as an accomplished fact and, using the past tense of the verb, declares that those He has justified He has already glorified.

Foreknown, predestined, called, justified, glorified — these are the five gold rings of the believer's security in Christ, the glorious heritage of all God's suffering children.

Have you ever seen the complete circle of a rainbow? I have experienced its glory only once. Never before had I realized that a rainbow is really a circle, for never before had I stood where its full expanse could be seen.

One brilliant winter day many years ago, I stood on the Canadian side of the Niagara River looking east towards the Rainbow Bridge that spans the gorge between Canada and United States. Beside me the escarpment dropped away in a sheer wall of rugged rock. Across from me the mighty cataract hurled its thundering waters into the seething cauldron below. Behind me the sun threw its afternoon radiance against the tides of spray rising ceaselessly from the boiling river. And circling far above me and below me, enclosing me in an arc of its luminous sweep, blazed the rainbow — a perfect circle of shimmering light, glowing with all the opalescence of the spectrum.

I gazed in silent awe. My heart bowed in wonder and adoration as I thought on the shining circle of sovereignty by which God links heaven and earth, Himself and His people, eternally together, within which His children suffer and triumph and rejoice in hope of the glory of God.

God set His bow in the cloud to remind mankind of His promise and His continuing care for His creation. We see it only as a small patch of light, or at best a partial arc, illuminating our stormy skies, but God tells us that the faint bow of promise we see so dimly is really a fragment of the eternal rainbow encircling His sovereign throne (Rev. 4:3, 10:1; Ezek. 1:26-28).

Foreknown, predestined, called, justified, glorified — what power can challenge the security of God's five gold rings? Paul asks this question in the closing verses in Romans 8.

• 43 •

THE ECHOING VOID

PICTURE A MAJESTIC MOUNTAIN PEAK TOWERING HIGH ABOVE all others, looking out in all directions across infinite vistas of space. Its loftiest pinnacle is crowned with an impregnable fortress. And there, safe within the shelter of God's sovereignty, His people dwell in peace and joy.

As Paul reflects on the unassailable security that is ours within the circle of God's five gold rings of promise, he seeks to express his inexpressible wonder. He can only break out in a rhetorical question: "What, then, shall we say in response to this?" For a moment the musing apostle sinks into silence, and then he posits five further questions (Rom. 8:31-39). Each is a challenge flung into the echoing void of the universe. Anyone may answer them who can. Our enemies, our adversaries in the invisible sphere of spiritual conflict, demons and fiends, principalities and powers, Satan himself — anyone who dares is invited to confront God's people and oppose their position in Christ. Yet as the questions are hurled into the abyss one after the other, their only answers are their own echoes. They reverberate into the immensity of space, only to die away at last into silence. No one rises to challenge the authority of God's people. Each of God's gold rings of security is matched by a question to which there can be no answer. What are these questions, and why are they unanswerable?

There can be no answer to the first question because of its opening words. *If God is for us, who can be against us?* Paul asks. *If God is for us,* the sovereign God of the everlasting covenant, the God whose Word to His people is sealed with the blood of His Son, if *this* God is for us — *and He is!* — what power in earth or hell can stand against us? Before the impact of this certainty, Satan and his hosts are dumb. The question goes echoing down the ages into silence.

The second question likewise is predicated on a strong statement of fact: Paul declares that *God did not spare His own Son, but gave Him up for us.* How then, he inquires, *will He not also, along with him, graciously give us all things?* Surely God will not deny His children anything we need when He has already given us His all in the unsurpassable gift of His Son! Once again, the echoes die away in the distance and the only answer to Paul's question is silence.

The statement that accompanies the third question holds the key to the silence that is its only answer. *Who will bring any charge against those whom God has chosen?* Paul asks. Certainly there are many who would like to do so. Sin, Satan, our foes, our own conscience — all of them could bring many charges against us. But wait! *It is God who justifies,* Paul declares, and God has acquitted us. We are His chosen children whom He has foreknown, predestined, called, and justified. If God Himself has declared us righteous in Christ Jesus, who then can dare to accuse us? The answer can only be dead silence.

But Paul continues his questioning. *Who is he that condemns?* he asks. Many might stand ready to answer this fourth question, for sin condemns us all. But once again comes God's mighty response to those who would pass judgment upon us: at His right hand *we have an advocate* interceding on our behalf — our crucified, risen, and exalted Savior. No one now can speak the word of condemnation against us. And so this question, too, rings out unanswered over the echoing void.

And finally, Paul comes to his last question. In Christ, God's people are secure from their foes, unthreatened by any lack of supply, safe from accusation, and free from fear of condemnation — but still there is more. *Who shall separate us from the love of Christ?* asks the apostle.

This time Paul does not give a response as he did with his previous questions: instead, he reviews a list of calamities that might seem to be able to shake our security in Christ: "Who shall separate us from the love of Christ?" he challenges us; "Shall trouble or hardship or persecution or famine or nakedness or danger or sword?" Any or all of these could have overtaken his readers; the same is true for us. But no, concludes Paul, such adversities can't harm us. In all these things we are more than conquerors through Him that loved us. Christ's love, which led Him to die for us, is sufficient to sustain us in all the sufferings of this life and to enable us to triumph even in death.

Paul's closing words of unshakable conviction are as true for us today as they were for the apostle and his first readers. They are the only words that can endure in the void of human suffering and echo back in joyous affirmation: "For I am convinced that neither death nor life, neither angels nor demons, neither the present nor the future, nor any powers, neither height nor depth, nor anything else in all creation, shall be able to separate us from the love of God that is in Christ Jesus our Lord." This is the power that enables God's children to suffer in faith and patience, and to be more than conquerors no matter what may come. All other words die away into silence, but the Word of our God lives and abides forever.

Is there an answer to the problem of human suffering? God does not answer all our questions any more than He answered Job's anguished cries. Rather, He reveals Himself in all His love and sovereignty to our suffering hearts and points us through the cross of Christ to our destiny of glory. There is God's answer to our suffering. In that glorious hope our trusting souls may rest.